Norwegian Patrol

DEDICATION

This book is dedicated to the aircrews of No. 233 General Reconnaissance Squadron, Royal Air Force; in particular to Air Commodore Ernest William Tacon, CBE, DSO, MVO, DFC, AFC, of Auckland, New Zealand — 'Bill' to the readers of this book — and to Sergeants 'Tubby' Davies and 'Gilly' Gilbert, DFM, wherever they may be.

It is also dedicated to my wife, Christine, who shared the rest of that long, long war with me and who encouraged me in the writing of this book and, lastly, to my brothers, Tudor of No. 88 Squadron, RAF and Teddy of the Royal Scots Greys, who did not return from that war.

Norwegian Patrol

Gron Edwards

Airlife
England

ISBN 0 906393 53 1

First published 1985
by Airlife Publishing Ltd.

Printed in England by Livesey Ltd., Shrewsbury.

Airlife Publishing Ltd.

7 St. John's Hill, Shrewsbury, England.

Contents

Foreword

Air Chief Marshal Sir Derek Hodgkinson, KCB, CBE, DFC, AFC

I knew Nos. 224 and 233 Squadrons well, as before the war I helped convert them from Ansons to Hudsons. I also knew the coast of Norway well as later, after the war had got under way, I rejoined my own Squadron — No. 220 Squadron — at Thornaby where we operated over the same geographical area as our sister Squadrons at Leuchars.

I mention this not just to prove my credentials, so to speak, in writing this Foreword, but so that the reader will know that I speak with some authority when I say that Gron Edwards has produced an accurate, perceptive and gripping account of a particularly hazardous and largely unsung epsiode of the 1939-45 war.

Central to the story is the fact that we were flying a civil airliner which had been converted into a military machine in the space of four days in 1938. The Lockheed Company which carried this out did a good job as the result was a vast improvement on the Anson — particularly in speed, radius of action and war load. However, there were two snags. First, the step from Anson to Hudson was a big one and many valuable Aircrew (and friends) were lost in the process of making it. Second, as we were soon to find out after the war had started, the Hudson operating at maximum range was no match at all to the Messerschmitt 109 and 110. Casualties were heavy and mounted alarmingly after the Germans invaded Norway. Morale took a knock and you can read in this book how prolonged operations involving heavy casualties can sap the will to fight. It was indeed only the determination and courage of people like Gron Edwards, Bill Tacon and their Crew, and there were enough of them in all Squadrons, who continued operating so long, that saved the day and enabled us to maintain the effectiveness of our patrols and offensive operations.

The book is, of course, enthralling to me as I can identify directly with almost every page. But, I think it will have a much wider appeal as it is well written with humour and a sure insight into the conditions of the day and life as a young man in the RAF at the beginning of the war.

June 1985

Chapter 1

The Cairo newspapers, in August 1939, had been full of the talk of war. Even the ship's newspaper mentioned the increasing international tension and I really wasn't in the mood for that sort of thing. Life was pleasant, sailing westward in the warm Mediterranean on board the comfortable P and O liner *Rawalpindi.* I ordered another gin sling from the deck steward and reflected that the life of a junior officer of the Royal Air Force was far from unpleasant. I had just delivered a Blenheim medium bomber to the RAF station at Helipolis, taking three days over the trip from England. The flying had been fun, I'd had a few good days in Cairo and was now, with the other members of the flight, on my way back to my squadron in the UK.

Bertie Mossford, of No. 269 Squadron, dropped into the deck-chair alongside me. 'Bit of a bugger, this Polish business, don't you think?'

'I'm not really thinking, Bertie. Life's far too pleasant here.'

'Yes, but Austria's gone, Czechoslovakia's gone and now it looks as though Poland's due for the chop. Tell you what. I think we'd be better keeping these Blenheims in England in case things blow up in Europe. We've still got some pretty obsolete aircraft at home and any old thing would do in the Middle East at the moment.'

Reluctantly, I returned to reality. Bertie was quite right, of course. It really did look ominous and I knew from my own squadron that we were in no fit state to carry out an effective war. I was in No. 233 Squadron stationed at Leuchars on the east coast of Scotland and our role was maritime reconnaissance. Our job would be to report on shipping movements through the North Sea between Scotland and Norway, to attack German ships and U-boats and to act as escort to our own ships moving in the area. In the Munich crisis last year we had been so unprepared for war that our aircraft were still painted in their peace-time silver livery, with squadron markings in bright enamel paints. An urgent order to remove all squadron markings and to camouflage the aircraft in the standard drab brown and green was greeted with dismay, followed by delight as it was discovered that the RAF was unable to supply the necessary paints. Our joy was short-lived, however; we were ordered to use ordinary household water-paint so our pretty aircraft disappeared for ever and we came to appreciate that it was just a very small incident in the trend towards more serious times ahead.

I approached these more serious times as many other 20-year-olds did, I suppose, by giving them as little thought as possible. Despite its rapid expansion, the RAF was still rather like a good club, small enough so that, when you flew about the country, there were few stations where you did not meet an old friend or acquaintance. We could take aircraft away on weekend leave, when the opportunity was usually taken to fly girl friends and relatives, smuggling them aboard in the voluminous Sidcot suits which we wore in an attempt to keep out the cold in our poorly heated aircraft. We had six weeks' leave a year. And we were all united in that we had joined the RAF for one reason only — we wanted to fly.

In 1936, when I had joined, we still flew biplanes and, though we liked technical advancement, we felt a little unsafe in the monoplane; it hadn't got a lot of nice wires that you could *see* were holding the aircraft together. And No. 233 Squadron's monoplane, the Anson, had a wooden wing that was very flexible and caused much apprehension in turbulent weather, when the thing creaked, groaned and rippled in a fashion that made you check that your parachute was handy. A few months ago, after a year of flying these new-fangled aircraft, I had felt that it was about time I cured myself of my fear of the monoplane and, though it was pushing things a bit, I felt that it would be a feather in one's cap to loop the loop in a twin-engined aircraft, an activity severely frowned upon by those in authority. I chose my time and flew about 20 miles away from Leuchars, where I wouldn't be seen, climbed to a fair height and, as a precaution in case the wings really *did* come off, put on my parachute pack. In twin-engined aircraft we wore the parachute harness but the pack itself was stowed in a rack close at hand and was clipped on when required. I felt that there was a possibility that it *might* be required. Clipped on to my chest, it got in the way of the controls a bit but not, I felt, enough to prevent me from flying the aircraft, an inaccurate assumption as it turned out.

I put the nose down, dived to get up plenty of speed and pulled the control column firmly back. She rose nicely into the loop but, as we approached the inverted position, the control column came into firm contact with the parachute pack and could come back no further. I had lost all elevator control and I was upside-down. I waited fearfully for the wrath to come and come it did. The Anson stalled and fell off the top of the loop like a ton of bricks. To the accompaniment of a massive creaking of protesting woodwork it thudded and crashed its way earthwards and, oh so slowly, completed the semblance of a loop at a speed well above its maximum permitted.

As the shrieking of the slipstream died away I took stock. My pulse rate had decreased to an acceptable twice-normal and I realised that the wings had, indeed, not come off. Not only had the Anson survived a stall but she had survived one upside-down, so it looked as though these monoplanes weren't so weak after all. I took off my parachute pack, re-stowed it, double-checked the grab handle of the emergency exit in the roof and the next loop was a doddle. With one more for luck I flew home a more confident pilot, wishing that I could pass on my knowledge to the other pilots of the squadron, but it could not be. I did not want to become a marked man. In the thirties one observed many of the conventions long since vanished; one behaved like an officer and a gentlemen (difficult to reconcile the two at times), at dinner one passed the port wine from right to left, on joining one's squadron one called upon the Commanding Officer's wife and, if she was in, solemnly presented her with one's visiting card. If she was not in one turned down one corner of the card and gave it to the servant, just why I have no idea. And, although it was not written down in so many words, one did not loop twin-engined aircraft because, even if you didn't pull the wings off it, you might strain it enough so that they fell off when the next pilot flew it.

Another secret which I kept throughout my service was my love of drilling on the barrack square. As a pilot it was expected of me that I despised the activity as quite irrelevant to our god-like existence in the air, but I was a shy and retiring character — 'Lacks personality' as one of my CO's confidential reports somewhat cruelly, but quite accurately, stated — and to be allowed to swagger and swing one's arms, marching and counter-marching, forming fours and moving to the left in column of fours, etc. was bliss to me, especially as we did it to the accompaniment of the best pipe band in the RAF. I had many a happy hour on the barrack square! But the air, of course, was my chief love as I left my lack of self-confidence behind when I got into an aircraft. The air was my element and I practised and experimented in every aspect of flying both theoretical and practical, and had been lucky enough to obtain an 'Exceptional' assessment as a pilot at my Flying Training School, a rather rare achievement. I also made a point of flying as many different types of aircraft as possible and had flown about twice as many types as most of the other pilots in 233 Squadron.

Bertie brought me back to reality again. 'Another John Collins, Dopey?' (I had acquired my nickname after the squadron had seen Walt Disney's *Snow White and the Seven Dwarfs* at the local cinema. It was suggested that there was a facial similarity between us and cast no aspersions on my mental capabilities, they said. Despite which it had taken some time to come to terms with it).

'Thanks, Bertie. I will. Look, Bertie, what do you really think about a war? What on earth can we do with Ansons against ships like the *Scharnhorst?*'

'Not a hell of a lot,' replied Bertie. 'Our hundred-pounders would hardly blow the paintwork off her and they certainly wouldn't penetrate the armour. Anyway, I think the situation wouldn't arise; we'd never get near her. She's stuffed full of anti-aircraft guns and they'd shoot us down like driven pheasants. And, again, I don't think the situation would arise as we couldn't, thank God, get to her.'

This was quite true; our role in war was to patrol the North Sea, but our Ansons hadn't got the range to get to Norway. There was a sixty-mile gap between the end of our planned patrol lines and the Norwegian coast, and all Germans ships slipping out of the Baltic would have a free run unless the Navy spotted them. And, by all accounts, the Luftwaffe were years ahead of us in aircraft production and outnumbered us greatly, so that we were going to have our hands full on a number of counts. All-in-all this really wasn't an ideal discussion subject for twenty-year-olds sunning themselves on the deck of a luxury liner.

'Remember that belly dancer in Cairo, Bertie?'

'Will I ever forget, is more the point. Coming for a swim?'

But, dismiss unpleasant thoughts as we did, we couldn't abolish the facts. Far sooner than we expected our world was to change. We did not know, then, that less than four months later, this great big *Rawalpindi's* flaming hulk would slide forever into the freezing coldness of the Iceland Channel as Captain Kennedy took her into forlorn action against the overwhelming might of the *Scharnhorst.* What we *did* know was that life was a great deal of fun.

I returned to my squadron on 8 August 1939 to find the station seething with excitement. We were to re-equip with a new type of aircraft. Built by Lockheeds, of Burbank, California, it was a military version of their fast Type 14 airliner and was to be called the 'Hudson'. It was of all-metal construction, had two 1,100 horse-power Wright Cyclone engines, was to have two fixed Browning machine-guns firing forward for the pilot to operate, two more in a 360 degree rotation turret in the mid-upper position and would carry 1,000 lbs of bombs. It had a top speed of 246 mph and unheard-of luxuries such as an automatic pilot and a cockpit-heating system that worked. (Our Ansons were agonisingly cold at altitude and in the winter.) This really was something — three times the horse power, two-and-a-half times the gun power, twice the range and five times the bomb load. There was only one snag. No. 224 Squadron, who shared Leuchars with us, were to get the Hudsons first and we would have to wait until they had converted.

The 'Flying Circus' arrived at Leuchars. Commanded by Squadron Leader Rankin, an Australian of exceptional keenness, it was the conversion training Flight. They flew in with a gaggle of dual-controlled Hudsons and got to work converting 224 Squadron; and it soon was obvious that there were problems, as aircraft started to crash and crews were killed. It was also obvious that the Hudson caught fire fairly easily and, when it did, its load of 536 gallons of petrol made a formidable blaze. Our enthusiasm became tempered with a great deal of respect for these powerful aircraft.

With the war fast approaching, 224 Squadron had already started their patrols across to the Norwegian coast in the hope of recording any German shipping movements out into the Atlantic, but they were, in fact, already too late. The pocket battleships *Graf Spee* and *Deutschland* had already slipped out on 21 and 24 August and our first casualty of the war occurred before its declaration. On 1 September Tinker Bell of 224 Squadron, on one of these patrols, hit a mountain in Norway in bad weather and all the crew were killed. In 233 we would be starting the war with our Ansons while converting simultaneously to Hudsons. A request that, as a precaution, we should fuse and load our bombs and belt up the tens of thousands of rounds of machine-gun ammunition required to fill our ammunition tanks was, incredibly, turned down by higher authority. As squadron Armament Officer, I felt that this was plain daft as it would take hours to get the squadron operational and we were expecting a blitzkrieg war to burst as suddenly upon us as it had burst upon Czechoslovakia and, now, Poland. One obeyed orders of course, so we continued converting to Hudsons until that historic Sunday, 3 September, when, at some ghastly hour of the morning, I was roused from sleep with the order to go ahead and arm up.

It was, of course, raining. In the soaking Scottish mist — the celebrated *haar* of the east coast of Scotland — we stood surrounded by a formidable amount of high explosive for which, to a man, we had the greatest respect. Our Armament Warrant Officer, Timber Woods, was the prime mover; I was just there to explain away any mistakes which we made, though mistakes in bomb fusing were frequently difficult to investigate owing to the tendency of those involved to disintegrate. The first bomb was brought into the fusing area and laid reverently down on the table; a 100 lb anti-submarine bomb, its yellow-painted body containing enough high explosive to blow us to Kingdom Come and we were suitably impressed. Timber Woods did the first one himself. Removing the transit plug from the nose he gauged the detonator pocket, carefully slid in the correct detonator and as carefully screwed in the nose pistol until it was tight down. The expected explosion did not occur and, slowly, the rest of us got into the swing of it. With the incentive of the continuous rain to help us, the bomb fusing was soon roaring along and it became apparent that a bomb, even a fused one, is a pretty innocuous object until you remove its safety devices. From that morning on they were treated carefully, of course, but not with kid gloves.

With the bomb fusing going well I checked the loading of a couple of sets on to the bomb racks of the first two aircraft and went over to the Armoury where, under cover, more fortunate armourers were belting up the Vickers gun ammunition and filling the drums for the Lewis guns. This was a laborious business, sorting out the four types of ammunition — ball, tracer, incendiary and armour-piercing — and belting them up in the correct sequence but, as it seemed to be going well, and as the Prime Minister was to speak to the nation at 11 a.m., I dashed back to the Mess in time to hear that we were, indeed, at war with Germany and then went back to the bomb dump. The hundred-pounders had all been fused by this time and they were working on the twenty-pounders. We could carry eight of these little horrors on our bomb racks but, fitted with instantaneous fuses as they were, they were quite useless against either shipping or submarines, being anti-personnel bombs. They were to have, however, a certain amount of effect on aircraft. *Our* aircraft, unfortunately.

The rain eventually cleared and I could report, soon after lunch, that the Ansons of 233 Squadron were ready to leap into the air in full fighting trim — two 100 lb A-S and eight 20 lb Cooper bombs on board, not to mention 300 rounds of Vickers and five 97-round Lewis drums. The Luftwaffe, had it known, may or may not have been impressed. By the end of the day we had fused up a complete reload and I could return to my quarters for a hot bath and the customary Sunday, though very belated, Pimms No. 1. Throughout the day the bad weather continued and there was no flying so, as I was stood down for the evening, I slipped into St. Andrews for a compulsive visit to my girl friend Joan. Joan was an art student at the Slade and was in the fortunate position of not having to live on herrings in a rat-infested garret. Her home was an extremely comfortable one in St. Andrews, her family marvellously hospitable and we had a deal of fun together but, alas, not on a very fiery plane as I obviously did not switch her on sexually. But the thought of dying on the morrow in the holocaust of war must have stirred up the adrenaline somewhat and, while I didn't stride into the family drawing room shouting *Moritui te salutamus,* whatever it was must have been equally ineffective and my proposal of marriage was turned down.

I returned to Leuchars on the last bus with my broken heart but with, too, a sense of relief. I don't think I *really* wanted to get married. I also felt that the Air Force might have a big job on its hands and that one thing at a time might be as much as could be managed by me for the moment. Because it looked as though we had, indeed, quite a job on hand. No. 224 Squadron had already had fatalities in training and, next day, we were to have our first. I had done a dual instruction flight on the Hudson and was in the Flight Office when I heard a change in the engine note of a Hudson that was taking off, followed by complete silence and then the thudding 'Whoomph' of exploding petrol. A Hudson had gone in.

I dashed out of the Flight Office to see a column of thick black smoke rising greasily from the river estuary beyond the edge of the aerodrome. As the fire engine started off I scrambled on board and we bumped and lurched across the grass to find that there wasn't a hope of survival for the crew: the tangled wreckage burned in the mud with an incredible roaring as a sea of fire, fed by 500 gallons of petrol, spread over the remains. All that showed of the aircraft through the rolling red torrent of smoke-laden flame were the tips of the wings and the rear fuselage, set at wildly irregular angles to each other. As we plunged into the knee-deep mud of the estuary to get to them we knew that it was useless and we had to wait for the flames to die down before the awful business started of getting the bodies out.

'Who is it?' I asked an airman slithering in the mud beside me.

'I don't know, sir, but it's a C Flight aircraft'.

A momentary relief that it wasn't a B Flight aircraft soon passed because I'd still know them well. I did. It was Robinson and Godfrey.

I'd always had a regard for Rob. One of our *enfants terribles,* always ready for a pint if anyone else was, he was efficient at work and, when I'd first joined the squadron two years earlier, he was a striking-looking chap with fair hair and contrasting brown eyes, a combination in a woman that sends you up the wall in two second flat. As I got to know him better his hair seemed to change somewhat and he became brindled and, eventually, dark-haired. I must have been staring at it once and wondering because he put his pint down and said, 'What the hell are you looking at?'

'Well, actually, Rob, it's you hair.'

'Oh, that? Have you got any cousins?'

'Three.'

'Girls?'

'Two of them.'

'So have I. Bloody little bitches,' he grinned. And he told his tale.

Three years earlier, before the RAF became known as the 'Brylcreem Boys', he had acquired an enormous bottle of Brylcreem from his barber; it must have been the original economy size and he was very proud of it. 'Paid for itself time and again, that bottle,' he used to say.

'Where's it now, Rob?' I asked.

'In the bloody bin, where it belongs,' said Rob. 'After a month I realised that my hair was going fair and I couldn't understand it. I got a bit suspicious when I was home on leave once as these cousins seemed to know all about it, kept tittering all the time. And then I screwed the truth out of them. ('Should have screwed the both of them at the same time, while I was at it,' he added darkly.) They'd put a cup of peroxide in my Brylcreem bottle, shaken it well up and left me to get on with the process of turning myself into an effing blonde.'

'Well, Rob, I must admit you did look a bit odd in the brindled stage,' I said.

He looked odder now, poor Rob, after the crash and ten minutes in that frightful fire. You couldn't tell which was him and which was Godfrey, the quiet, studious Canadian who had already taken his examinations to be an airline pilot while we lighter-hearted types read the *Daily Mirror* with a tankard at our sides. The firemen had got the foam apparatus across to the wreckage; we slipped and slithered in the combined mud and foam, got the bodies on to stretchers and brought them ashore. It was about a mile across the aerodrome to the tarmac so I walked back to clear my head. It looked as though these Hudsons were going to take a lot of handling. To jump from the easy Anson to a machine with three times the horse power and a highly tapered wing with its more violent stalling characteristics was going to be a big step.

We worked out why Rob and Godfrey had crashed. The tail trimming wheel on the Anson was mounted in the fore-and-aft plane and worked as one would expect it to; it was wound clockwise to trim the aircraft tail-heavy, and *vice versa,* a natural movement. In the Hudson the wheel was mounted at right angles to the fore-and-aft plane so that one already had to re-think the movement and, unfortunately, it was designed to operate in the opposite way to which an Anson pilot would have wound it by instinct. The trimming wheel on the wreck was found wound fully tail-heavy. It looked as though the trim had been a bit on the tail-heavy side at take-off and that the pilot had trimmed it a bit more nose-heavy in the Anson manner, thus making things worse. And the more he 'corrected' the worse it got. The machine had taken off into an immediate climb that even the full strength of the pilot couldn't alter as he tried to push the control column forward against the immensely powerful trimming tab on the elevator. At 100 feet the left wing dropped in a vicious stall and she dived into the estuary.

We were starting to learn the hard way. We all had great respect for the Hudson with its power, quick stall, powerful flaps, etc. Everything about it was bigger and faster and more powerful than anything we were used to and it took time to come to terms with it. The day had yet to come (though it would) when I would fling it about and just use it as a tool of the trade. When that day did come I still retained my respect for the aircraft and it repaid me by turning out to be a first-class machine that would absorb a lot of punishment and still get you home.

Our conversion course was well run by the Travelling Circus, the comprehensive course of lectures all well planned. With a chart of the hydraulic and fuel systems pinned to the board the instructor would lay the tip of his pointer somewhere in the writhing mass of pipelines and say 'A Messerschmitt 109 has just put a bullet into the system *there.* What's going to happen? Equally important, what is not going to happen that you would like to happen?'

And you had to work it out. 'Well, I think you would be able to open your bomb doors but I don't think you can get your flaps down for landing.'

'And what about your landing gear?'

'Well, I think you'd have to use the emergency hand pump to get that down.'

'You *think?* Look, you've got to *know.* That 109 put a bullet through a petrol tank as well, so you're short of fuel, night has fallen and you need to know whether to get weaving with the hand pump when you're five miles out, not when you're sweating it out six feet off the deck. Now, *will* your landing gear come down or not?'

And so on. It was good training, but it still didn't stop the accidents. By modern standards we were obviously rushed as I checked out solo after 2 hours 40 minutes dual and I don't suppose that that is much, really, for a machine packing over 2000 horse power. Still, it was all we got so we had to make do with it. There was an urgency to get both squadrons operational so as to close the sea passage across to Norway as effectively as possible, but whether the accidents as a result of our rushed training were justified by the increased efficiency of our patrols nobody could guess. It was a fairly typical example of service flying that was repeated in all the air forces of the world, always had been and probably always would be.

Concurrently with our training we patrolled in our Ansons, escorting coastal convoys and heading out towards Norway, though we had to leave a large unsearched gap ahead of us as we turned for home. On the third day of the war, Yorke, of A Flight, had found a U-boat on the surface and had swept in to the attack. After giving it the two 100 lb anti-submarine bombs he roared in and gave it the eight twenty-pounders for luck. Fused, alas, with their instantaneous fuses they went off on the surface with a hell of a crump and riddled his petrol tanks with tiny fragments. He came screaming home at full throttle before he lost all his petrol and made a good landing not *too* far from the aerodrome. As he streaked up the Eden estuary his engines quit cold and he splashed down into the water, getting ashore in the rubber dinghy. After a triumphant de-briefing in the Operations Room he reappeared in the Mess and the beer flowed as he went through the action time and again. This was war! This was fun!

And then the phone rang. 'Would Pilot Officer Yorke please report to the Operations Room.' Later he came back somewhat chidden. It hadn't been a U-boat, it had been one of our submarines — *Seahorse* — shaken up but none the worse. And another Anson from another squadron had done the same thing to another submarine the same day. The Navy were displeased and an inter-service argument raged. Both submarine commanders said that they were in submarine sanctuaries (areas where our subs could surface for battery charging without being attacked, the sanctuary being marked on all our charts). Both the RAF pilots said they were outside the sanctuary. Submarine navigation is notoriously difficult and frequently inaccurate (by Guess and by God the submariners called it) but the incidents led to a tightening up of ideas and to a parade in the Firth of Forth a day later when three different classes of submarine sailed up and down while plane-loads of pilots circled round them improving on their ship recognition.

The day I checked out on the Hudson I was on standby duty. I'd just got into the Mess for lunch when I was dragged off to the Ops Room with Sgt Axe. A U-boat had been sighted in the Firth of Forth. 'Not blooming *Seahorse* again, I hope,' I muttered at the Controller. 'No, a U-boat, get cracking.'

Sgt Axe and I shot into the air and streaked over to the sighting area, getting about 145 knots out of the Anson at full throttle. We thought we saw something that could look like a U-boat that had submerged so we gave them our earth-shaking 100-pounders. Nothing happened. Just to let them know that the ever-vigilant RAF were there we dropped a couple of twenty-pounders. They'd make a bang and keep a U-boat down while we went back for lunch. They also made a goodly crump, though we dropped them from a reasonable height. I became a respector of the instantaneous fuse. No wonder Yorke had copped it two days earlier.

For the next month we alternated 4½-hour patrols in our Ansons north-eastwards towards Norway, with continuing training on our Hudsons. During this period I had a go at flying underneath the River Tay railway bridge. It was also a period when I was starting to get to know a new boy in the squadron — Bill Tacon, from New Zealand. Bill had been posted to B Flight and I was at a peculiar stage of my career when, because of my youth, I was still regarded by many as 'the lad'. At the same time it had to be admitted that I had a fair amount of experience, over 700 hours, and, because of my habit of scrounging different types of aircraft wherever I went, I had flown many more different types of aircraft than any other junior officer in the squadron — I had twelve different types in my log book. Cooper, my Flight Commander, alternated with placing me as second pilot to older pilots with less actual experience than I had, to making me first pilot with a sergeant as second pilot. It was a system I didn't like. Most of the chaps with whom I flew as second pilot were a bit selfish and did all the flying themselves, making me navigate every trip. I wasn't in favour of the officer/sergeant team as the two pilots were in different messes and so didn't communicate in off-duty hours. One learned a lot and built up a better team by nattering the eternal shop which we all talked in the mess. I was in favour of the pilots being either two officers or two sergeants. One day I was dignified with the job of first pilot with Bill Tacon as second pilot and it was my turn to fly. It was the first of what were to be many trips with Bill and, when we became an officially paired crew, we flew turn and turn about. On this particular day we had just done a 4½-hour patrol in an Anson and had landed at Montrose to refuel. As we flew south I said to Bill, 'Remember the Fleet Air Arm Lieutenant who was in the mess the other day? You know, with a beard and flying a Steam Chicken[1]. Rather elderly.'

'I think so,' said Bill. 'About 30 years old.'

'That's him,' I said. 'Well, he once flew a Flycatcher under the Tay Bridge.'

We flew silently on. Arbroath passed beneath the starboard wing. 'Leuchars in seven minutes,' said Bill. 'You mean the Forth Bridge, don't you?'

'No, the Tay Bridge.'

Carnoustie came up and I brought the Anson down for a spot of low flying along the beach at Duddon Ness. I lifted a wingtip over a rising sand dune and slid down the other side.

'Quite neat,' said Bill. 'Couldn't do it any better myself. But it's a very *small* bridge, isn't it?'

'A bit on the small side, I think. Our wing span is 56 feet and we're 13 feet from wheels to the top of the wireless mast,' I said.

[1]Steam Chicken — the Walrus amphibian. Also known as a Shagbat.

'Oh yeah, been doing your homework', said Bill. 'What's the span of the bridge'.

'I'm not quite sure, Bill. But enough.'

'And its height?'

'Again, I'm not quite sure but it's low tide now, you know; that gives us more space.'

'Well, that's something, I suppose,' said Bill. 'But a Flycatcher was a pretty small aircraft wasn't it? I'll bet it didn't span more than 30 feet. Still it's more or less on our way home. No harm in having a look at it, I suppose.'

We nipped across Buddon Ness and flew low up the River Tay. As we approached the bridge I must say that, from a mile away, it looked a bit on the small side. I eased the Anson slowly closer to the water and lined up on the middle of the bridge. As we got closer, at about 400 yards, I looked through the gun sight to find that we had a lot of starboard drift on with the southerly wind, so I turned left and crabbed her in towards the bridge. Every detail of the massive steel girderwork was now rushing at us at 120 knots; it looked an enormously solid structure and the span didn't seem all that big. Our drift to starboard now looked rather alarming and I was so low that I couldn't do a banked turn in case I put the port wingtip into the water. I flat-turned her with left rudder to try and get rid of that worrying starboard drift, not with complete success, and the available space between the water and that horrible-looking monster of steel, with its massive piers and criss-cross girders, didn't seem so very much bigger than the amount of airspace which we, ourselves, occupied. An awful thought struck me. Maybe it was *high* tide, in which case there was 25 feet less than I thought I'd got, and I found myself becoming distinctly worried. I could now see every detail of the bridge. 'Time they gave it a coat of paint,' I thought, but that harassing degree of drift just wouldn't go away and, low tide or high, I didn't feel I could get her under without our propellers hitting the water. I broke. I heaved back on the stick with all my might and we shot over the top of the bridge, missing by about a couple of coats of paint.

'Chicken!' said Bill. 'Mind you, it's about time you came to your senses.'

'You can't win 'em all, Bill. Let's get on with the ruddy war.'

Joan had been getting on with *her* war in the meantime. She rang me up. 'I've joined the WAAFs[1], Dopey,' she said.

[1]Woman's Auxiliary Air Force.

My heart sank. I still nursed a secret hope that I'd swing her round. 'When do you go?' I asked.

'Tomorrow, I'm to do my initial training as an MT Driver.'

Hell, I was on Standby aircraft and couldn't leave the station. 'Well, try and get yourself posted to Leuchars when you finish the course,' I said.

'I'll try,' said Joan in a not altogether convincing tone. 'Goodbye, Dopey. Good luck.'

'And to you, Joan. See you on leave sometime. Goodbye.' But, if I knew anything about the Air Force, they'd post her to Cornwall.

The conversion to Hudsons was progressing. No. 224 Squadron were now fully operational on the Norwegian beat and we did in-shore escorts for the north- and south-bound convoys running out of the Firth of Forth. There were occasional submarine scares and special investigations of specific vessels to do and, in the meantime, we continued with our conversion course. As with all new equipment there were snags and shortages, one of the most serious shortages being in our gunnery equipment. There was a dearth of firing gear for our front Browning machine-guns, which were fired pneumatically, and we had very few of the Boulton-Paul turrets for the mid-upper position. These were fitted as soon as they arrived from the manufacturers but if an aircraft hadn't got its turret yet we carried a large steel plate, bolted over the gun mounting, as ballast. Without the turret the machine was a good ten knots faster but the majority of us preferred the presence of that big, fat, air-resistant turret and its two Brownings, which also gave us a gunner with 360 degree all-round look-out capability.

On 10 October I did my first operational trip in a Hudson in a machine without a turret and, at the last moment, our Air Officer Commanding, Air Commodore Breese, had hopped aboard. We slipped quickly across to Norway, noting all shipping movements, and on the way home we met up with a balloon that had obviously broken away from one of the east coast barrages. We'd seen these things burn at the pre-war Hendon air displays and we swept down intending to set fire to it with the front guns but the gun-firing system went on the blink and the Brownings wouldn't work. The only gun in the aircraft that *would* work was my .38 Enfield revolver so I opened the side window to have a (quite useless, but rather fun) crack at it with the pistol, but the Air Commodore turned down the idea in case I hit a propeller blade with a bullet. Slightly chidden, I retired to my navigation table in the nose and unloaded the pistol as we flew on home, now in continuous rain and low cloud, which made flying hazardous and navigation more difficult. I aimed to show up well in front of the Air Commodore and managed to make an impressively accurate landfall at Fife Ness and we landed as the low cloud started to clamp down. During the day visibility decreased even further and it degenerated into a pig of a night. Mike Clarke and Lockley of C flight, returning from a later patrol, flew into a hill covered by the low cloud and all four crew were killed, the aircraft catching fire, as usual.

They always seemed to catch fire. Four days earlier I had been out for a walk when I saw a 224 Squadron Hudson taking off. When it was about 500 feet up it looked as though a giant had reached out and got hold of the left wingtip. The right wing reared up, the aircraft flicked on to its back and dived earthwards in an immediate spin. To see so large an aircraft whirled through the air like an autumn leaf at that speed was awe-inspiring and frightening and I heard a protesting 'No!' come from my lips as the machine spun its fatal way to earth and four more men died. A couple of seconds after it vanished behind some trees came the familiar 'Whoomph' and the greasy black smoke welled upwards. I didn't bother going across to the crash. There wasn't a hope for anyone on board and Rob and Godfrey's affair in the mud of the estuary had cured me of hopeless causes.

About a week after Mike Clarke bought it I was on an early patrol, with Sgt Hallam as navigator. It had been a misty night with a hard frost and we arrived at dispersal to find the Hudson entirely covered with thick hoar frost, so thick that it was immediately detectable in the darkness, in the flickering lights of the ground crews' torches. I knew enough about aerodynamics to know that the most important part of the wing of an aircraft, that part that yields the majority of the lift, is the upper surface of the wing just back from the leading edge. By the time we had assessed the state of the aircraft and obtained a couple of yard brushes to sweep the wing we were already late for take-off so I made do with brushing the frost off an area for about three feet back from the leading edge of the wing and left the rest for our de-icing systems to cope with later.

As rapidly as possible we taxied out, rolled down the runway at full throttle and got airborne but, before I could start the retraction of the undercarriage, the remaining runway lights stretching ahead of me started to slide over to the right, vanished, and the disorientation started as we flew into the pitch-black morning. The speed was dangerously low and would not build up; a quick glance at the artificial horizon on the instrument panel showed me to be in a climbing turn to the left. A rumbling vibration now shaking the aircraft indicated that the left wingtip was trailing along the ground and I was obviously completely stalled. The instinctive reaction of winding on right aileron was only going to make things worse so I rammed on full right rudder and put the port engine throttle right through the gate into emergency boost; we were obviously in serious trouble. Out of the corner of my eye I became aware of Sgt Hallam leaving the cockpit for a safer place and didn't blame him one little bit, as he could give me no assistance at all; there just wasn't anything else I could do, except wait and pray, to get this bucket of trouble into the air. After that it would be difficult to say which registered first: the shocking, violent impact; the shrieking, rending screech of tearing metal; or the aviator's nightmare, the explosive 'Whoof' and the enormous orange flame as the petrol went up. The rest, as Hamlet said, was silence. I took no more conscious part in the proceedings for a while . . .

It was dark and rather cold but the sensation of undulation was pleasant. A voice, which I thought could be that of Sgt Hallam, said 'Come on, you clot (only it wasn't 'clot', it was a cruder and more basic four-letter word) we've got to get out of this.'

I wondered to whom he was talking as he was being extremely rude. In the meantime I continued to revel in the delightful, wavy motion which fitted the Barcarole from the *Tales of Hoffman* to perfection. He'd got something, had old Offenbach — Tum, te tum; and rise and fall; and uuuundulate; togeeeether. Great!

'Come on, you clot, we've got to get out of this.' The person whom Sgt Hallam was addressing was obviously proving obstructive.

The movements ceased to be soothing and undulating and became rough and violent. I was flung hard and painfully against an unyielding object and demanded of the invisible world around me what the hell was up.

'You're on top of me,' said Hallam's voice. 'We're jammed under the wireless operator's seat and until you get off me neither of us can get out.'

'If we're under the wireless operator's seat,' I asked Hallam reasonably, 'where's the wireless operator?'

'How the hell should I know?' snarled Hallam mutinously. 'He's probably mixing it with the gunner back in the turret. Now will you, for Chrissakes, get off me.' 'Sir,' he added. Knew which side his bread was buttered, now.

I wriggled about and extricated myself and gave Sgt Hallam a hand out. The floor of the aircraft seemed to be on a slope and, in the darkness, two dim forms made themselves known to me, the wireless operator and the gunner.

'Where the dickens are we?' I asked.

'I think we're in the estuary, sir,' said the gunner. 'The back of the cabin is under water. We'll have to wade ashore.'

We stumbled down the sloping cabin floor, pushed open the door and slid down carefully into the murk. The icy water only came up to our chests so we'd be O.K. We turned towards the tail end and waded along the side of the fuselage, our feet dragging and sticking in the gooey mud of the estuary but, the further we went, the deeper became the water. 'There must be a gully here,' someone opined, then the darkness was banished in a brilliant white light as someone on the aerodrome fired a flare. As we looked ahead we could see nothing but estuary stretching away into the limit of visibility. 'The aerodrome's behind us,' called the gunner and, sure enough, it was. We could now see that the Hudson had gone into the river backwards, having spun right round. In walking towards the tail we'd been walking further out into the estuary. We turned and waded back, climbing up the steep bank to the aerodrome twenty feet above and got into the ambulance. My next memory is of being in Sick Quarters with the Medical Officer giving us the once-over and I remember apologising to the crew. 'Sorry, chaps,' I muttered. 'God, Hallam, you do look a sight.'

'Taken a good look at yourself, recently?' asked Hallam.

I'd asked my batman to press my trousers the previous afternoon. Alas, I'd undone his good work. Our uniforms were soaked and torn and our trousers were mud from the knees down. I staggered off to my quarters and climbed into bed. Far too soon I was awakened by Britten, my batman, coming noisily into the room as he was expecting me to be away flying. When he saw my inert form he stopped and quietened down. I opened half an eye and saw him look at my uniform with horror. He stared at the ruins of his work and shook his head in sorrow. Experienced RAF batman that he was he knew that it must have been a hell of a party but, really, what *was* the world coming to? I made a mental note to give him half a crown and fell asleep again.

I went down to Flights in the afternoon to sort things out. With the entire aircraft covered in a sort of rough fur coat of hoar frost the aerodynamic drag had been tremendous and had prevented the speed from building up. The poor airflow over the wings, despite our sweeping some of the frost off, had resulted in the left wing stalling and dropping to the ground while the right wing rose further and further into the air. We were heading for the estuary, to dive straight into it in another fatal crash at just the spot where Rob and Godfrey had bought it six weeks before — only the gods were kind. Our left wing went straight into an Anson parked on the perimeter, completely wrecking it. The Anson got its own back, by tearing off our left wing and engine, the ruptured petrol tanks releasing 250 gallons of petrol to be ignited by the exhaust flame and the impact swung us round like a catherine wheel to go backwards into the estuary, the water putting the fire out. All-in-all, about as neat a solution to our problems as you could possibly wish for. While I wasn't up to the standard of the tailor of the fairy tale who got seven at one blow, two wasn't to be sneezed at. It's still a squadron record. On the credit side, all aircraft on early detail in similar climatic conditions were subsequently kept nice and warm in the hangars overnight.

There was to be a Court of Enquiry into the accident, of course, and I sensed an air of censure from above. I felt a bit resentful of this as, while I wouldn't have dreamed of flying an aircraft in such a state in peace-time, one aircraft missing from a patrol left a large gap in the pattern, the commerce raiders of the Germany Navy were very active and were sinking a lot of our shipping in the North and South Atlantic. Indeed, nobody had ever seen an aircraft in such a state in peace-time and I reckoned that I'd been fairly well on the ball in sweeping at least *some* of the wing clear of frost as even that action had put me a quarter of an hour late in getting off. As Sgt Hallam and I worked on our statement, however, a report came in from No. 8 Flying Training School at Montrose, thirty miles up the coast, that they had had a similar experience. Even after waiting for daylight to begin their flying training they had had three similar, though milder, stalls on take-off and one of the Oxfords, emulating me, had sat down like a broody hen on another parked machine. It looked as though I wasn't the only B.F. on the coast. The enquiry, after that, was minimal.

There remain, however, 20 minutes lost from my life. Amnesia after concussion is a strange thing. I remember climbing up out of the estuary and getting into the ambulance. The next thing I remember is being stripped to the waist in the Sick Quarters with the rest of the crew and talking to the Medical Officer. I seemed to come back to reality in the middle of a conversation and nobody was staring at me in such a way as to indicate that my actions were in any way peculiar, so I must presume that, to the outside world, I was in every way normal during this period. And I was as unaware, myself, that anything peculiar had happened, never having heard of amnesia. Had anyone asked me what it was, I'd have plumped for its being a name of a female in Arthur Askey's popular radio show, probably a friend of Nausea Bagwash. You may well say that I deserved to get stunned when I was flung into the radio compartment as I was obviously not strapped in to my seat and, maddeningly, it had been the only occasion in my flying career when I had not done so. In the hassle of getting our delayed aircraft into the air it was the one bit of my cockpit check that I'd omitted. As the amnesia didn't exist as far as I was concerned, it didn't worry me, of course. Britten washed out and re-pressed my uniform, I spent an uncomfortable few days with a headache, and pronounced aches from head to foot, and then all returned to normal.

Chapter Two

In November the Luftwaffe started bombing our trawlers in the North Sea, which caused a great deal of indignation throughout the country, in which we aircrew joined. We claimed that the trawlermen were non-combatant civilians and the Germans said that maybe they were, but they were suspected of reporting the movements of any German aircraft they saw, which was, I suppose, a distinct possibility. The trawlers were, of course, bringing essential food into Britain and, as such, were as much a legitimate target in total warfare as were the merchant ships which were getting such a pounding in the North Atlantic, but the emotional side of the affair was well played on by our propaganda people and we all ignored what we did not want to know and joined in the (quite genuine) feeling of horror aroused by the bombing and machine-gunning of small, unarmed ships. Some day we'd get our own back on the Luftwaffe.

The chance came at the end of November when Bill Tacon and I were returning home on a parallel track search. We had gone down to sea level to check on a small Norwegian merchant vessel named the *Bruse* and were climbing away to rejoin our patrol line when the Hudson came alive to the cry of 'Enemy aircraft ahead. Flying low over the water.' I put the gun button to 'Fire', thumbed a quick squirt to test my guns and swept down upon it. It was a Dornier 18K flying boat and it was going to be a difficult full-deflection shot as he was pointing at right angles to me. As I dived I gave him a ring and a half deflection on the gunsight and prepared to start my left turn to keep the sight bearing. I didn't have to, as he wasn't moving. He was *on* the water. I withheld my fire, swept over him and returned for another look, our gunner keeping the turret trained on him all the time. The Dornier seemed to be in good shape, some of the crew were outside on the top decking and neither of the gun positions seemed to be manned, though we kept a wary eye on them. After a more careful examination it looked, in fact, as though she was settling by the stern. We kept taking photographs of her and eventually decided she was sinking. The North Sea in winter is a damned cold place so we went back to the *Bruse,* talked to her with our Aldis lamp and persuaded her to come back and pick up the Dornier crew, after which we did some target practice on the aircraft with our machine-guns to accelerate her sinking, keeping some ammunition in reserve in case we met up with anything else on the remainder of the patrol. After landing we went to the Ops Room. The Station Commander was there and heard our report.

'You got the crew picked up? What on earth for? Why didn't you drop a bomb on them and blow them to bits?' he asked.

'Sir,' I cried in horror. 'You can't do a thing like that.'

'Oh, yes, you bloody well can,' said the Groupie.

'Hardly cricket, sir,' I countered.

'In case you've forgotten, Dopey,' he said, 'It isn't cricket we're playing. It's war. What price your trawlers now?'

Bill and I left the Ops Room in a confused state of mind. 'Bet *he* wouldn't bomb chaps on the water?' said Bill.

'Yet he's got a point, you know,' I said. 'That bunch will find some way of getting out of their internment in Norway (how right I was to be) and, when they get back to the Luftwaffe, they'll be shadowing our ships and homing in the bombers on them again.'

We walked in silent thought towards the Mess, where tea would soon be on. 'Look, Bill,' I broke the silence, 'Life isn't all cricket and cucumber sandwiches, you know. We'll have to take tougher action in future.'

'Yes,' said Bill, rather unconvincingly I thought, 'We'll do that.' And added, after a pause, 'You know, Dopey, I've never had a cucumber sandwich.'

That's the worst of being a New Zealander, you do tend to miss out on things.

We had to grow up some time, I suppose, but it would be a long time before the air service lost its fellow-feeling for the opposition. After all, it might be us down there in the freezing drink one day. That I must have been pretty juvenile in those days is shown by the following letter. Apart from the jolly hockey sticks approach to air combat it wasn't really the most considerate letter you could send to a mother who already had three sons in the fighting services. And talk about security! I'm sure that the German Intelligence Service would have loved to have handed the letter over for Haw-Haw on Radio Zeesen to have a ball with.

Leuchars,
21/9/39

Dear Mother,

Things are carrying on pretty quietly now and seem too peaceful for a war. The training on Hudsons is getting on quite well and I am theoretically fully qualified on them. They take quite a deal of management, and one is quite busy doing circuits on them, especially so as the aerodrome is pretty well carved up by men working on concrete runways and levelling. What available landing space there is is taken up the whole time. Once one is used to them they are quite nice to handle although the aileron control is much the same as an American car as it is so low geared. The wheel can be turned right over whereas in the Anson it can be turned through 60 degrees only which gives much more positive control, and which is much better, as the only time one really needs full aileron is in an emergency or when fighting and it is a great nuisance to have to fly hand over hand when one has other things to think about. We have been doing quite a deal of patrols over the North Sea and some fellows have had the luck to meet a German flying boat with whom they had an argument. Both sides did some quite good shooting.

It is a shocking business about the *Courageous,* isn't it?

About six of our fellows have married in the last three weeks. I would rather like to do it but I don't think it is advisable, as two fellows I know who were married some time ago have been killed, so I suppose I shall stay single.

I hope you are all quite well. I am enjoying myself quite well.

Love

Gron

P.S. Some more stamps. The last of the batch.

As 1939 came to an end both 233 and 224 Squadrons had become fully operational. Whereas in the early days we had flown without gun turrets, with defective front gun-firing systems and a host of other teething troubles, our full equipment gradually arrived and the problems were overcome. The day came when we sent away the last of our Ansons to a unit still using them and were declared fully operational with 18 first-line aircraft and six in reserve. Bad weather and accidents continued to take their toll as in the cases of Tinker Bell and Mike Clarke. Sgt Hallam, who had survived the brief, twenty-second flight into the Eden estuary with me in October, crashed in bad weather in South Wales while testing out the new airborne ASV (Anti-surface-vessel) radar with which we were soon to be equipped, and all the crew were killed. McLaren and Evans, after getting airborne, retracted their undercarriage just a little too soon. The heavily laden Hudson sank down again, the airscrews hit the ground and the flight came to an abrupt end as the machine skated along the runway on its belly and hit a large electrical transformer, catching fire immediately. The crew scrambled out, shaken but unhurt, and after a few minutes of the roaring heat from 500 gallons of burning petrol, the bombs cooked off and went up with an almighty bang, blowing the Hudson to smithereens.

The almost automatic fire which followed any major Hudson crash was due to the design of the petrol system. In all the previous aircraft we had flown the petrol tanks were separate units fixed in various convenient locations in the wings and fuselage. In the Hudson considerable weight had been saved by using the metal skin of the wing as the tank itself. Each wing root, where it joined the fuselage, was made petrol-tight in two separate tanks holding 125 and 143 gallons respectively, a total tankage of 536 gallons, which gave us a safe endurance of seven hours or so. Only a few feet away from these tanks were the large exhaust pipes of the 1100 hp Cyclone engines, which belted out a considerable flame at full throttle. Any shock large enough to strain the rivetting of the wing surfaces would automatically lead to a petrol leak. In impacts such as McLaren's and mine, where we hit heavy objects at speed, it was understandable that the wing surface would disintegrate and lead to an immediate, explosive fire but what was a bit more worrying was that a relatively mild accident, such as an undercarriage broken in a heavy landing or through enemy gunfire, could also lead to a serious fire. As the undercarriage leg collapsed the wingtip hit the ground and the strain on the stressed-skin construction of the wing could be enough to open up the rivetting on its undersurface — and out came the petrol to be ignited either by the exhaust flame or by sparks caused by friction on the runway from the broken undercarriage leg.

A second source of fire lay in the large electric battery which we carried. It was a truly beefed-up job which made the Hudson independent of an external battery when starting up the engines, a considerable advantage when you'd had to land away from base, and it was mounted down in the belly of the aircraft. If this battery got a good clout, as in a heavy belly-landing, it got pushed upwards and short-circuited itself against the metal floorboards above it. There was enough power in the battery to set these alight and a modification was eventually introduced to reduce the chances of this happening, but the fear of fire persisted in our minds for some time.

Throughout the winter the squadron was quietly busy. Every shipping movement in the North Sea was investigated, escorts supplied to naval ships and convoys, offensive patrols sent out to trouble spots, rescue aircraft sent to torpedoed and sinking ships. Occasionally we met German reconnaissance aircraft, usually the Dornier 18K or Heinkel 115 and sporadic combats ensued. You can't expect too much drama in combats between twin-engined reconnaissance aircraft, not the stirring stuff of the fighter boy in his Hurricane or Spitfire. Trained to do one job in a machine designed for one job only, the fighter boy frequently got his man. We had other things to do; shooting was only a small part of our training and our machines were much larger and heavier, and consequently not so handy. Despite this we had our moments. The first German aircraft to be shot down in the war was a Dornier 18K shot down by a Hudson of 224 Squadron from Leuchars on 8 October 1939.

We also attacked U-boats, though not with great success. For some reason anti-submarine attacks had formed no part of our peacetime training. We trained entirely in reconnaissance and bombing but with no accent on the incredibly difficult target that the diving U-boat was to present. It was obvious that one would have to aim a stick of bombs ahead of the last known position of the U-boat but it was a hit-and-miss business, chiefly miss. In the opaque waters of the North Sea, once the conning tower had vanished from sight it was as though that big black boat had never been there. The conning tower slick vanished in seconds and then there was nothing but the tossing waves and the fearful knowledge that, not many yards away and not many feet beneath you, a thousand tons of lethal craft manned by an enemy had slid to safety as you flew impotently over him. We had no special bombsight, depth charges or other technical gear, just aim by eye and drop bombs with contact fuses. The fuse was ignited by the impact with the water and had a preset delay to get it down to what was guessed as the most likely effective depth before it exploded, but the later hydrostatic pistol of the aircraft depth-charge was much more efficient.

An event which passed largely unnoticed that winter was my 21st birthday. Bill Tacon and I had taken off in the morning for

Self in photograph of Hart Trainer. Taken in Sywell in November 1936.

A page from my log book with which I am quite chuffed. Not many Exceptional ratings were dished out. It will support my claim that I was christened 'Dopey' on account of appearance only, and not because of limitations as to my mental capabilities.

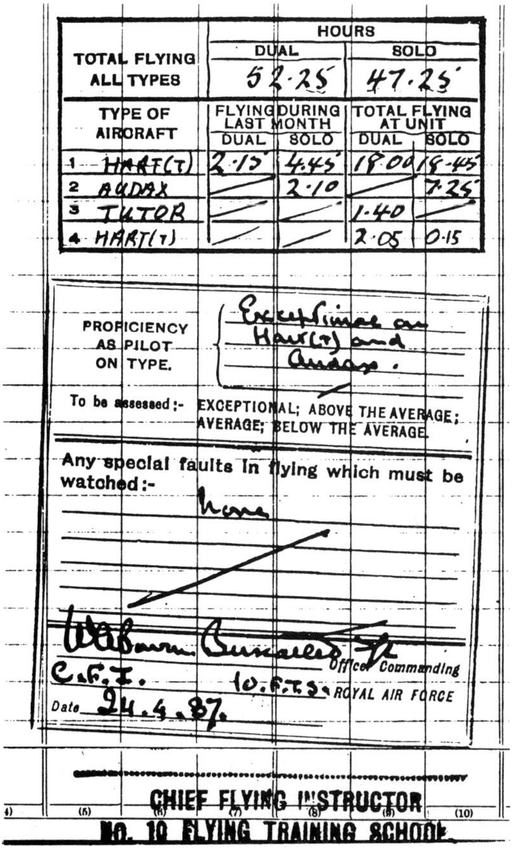

TOTAL FLYING ALL TYPES	HOURS DUAL	HOURS SOLO
	52·25	47·25

TYPE OF AIRCRAFT	FLYING DURING LAST MONTH DUAL	FLYING DURING LAST MONTH SOLO	TOTAL FLYING AT UNIT DUAL	TOTAL FLYING AT UNIT SOLO
1 HART(T)	2·15	4·45	18·00	18·45
2 AUDAX	—	2·10	—	7·25
3 TUTOR	—	—	1·40	—
4 HART(T)	—	—	2·05	0·15

PROFICIENCY AS PILOT ON TYPE. Exceptinal on Hart(T) and Audax.

To be assessed:- EXCEPTIONAL; ABOVE THE AVERAGE; AVERAGE; BELOW THE AVERAGE.

Any special faults in flying which must be watched:- None

[illegible] Officer Commanding

C.F.I. 10. F.T.S. ROYAL AIR FORCE

Date 24.4.37.

CHIEF FLYING INSTRUCTOR

NO. 10 FLYING TRAINING SCHOOL

No. 233 Squadron Anson in pre-war silver colours. On the fifth day of the war the author dropped his first bombs from one of these aircraft on a suspected U-Boat in the Firth of Forth.

From the left: Sgt. Gilbert, Air Gunner; Author; Bill Tacon; Sgt. Tubby Davies, Wireless Operator, who, obligingly, used to eat most of my sandwiches.

Lockheed 'Hudson'

Hudson Cockpit. (I.W.M.)

Sinking.

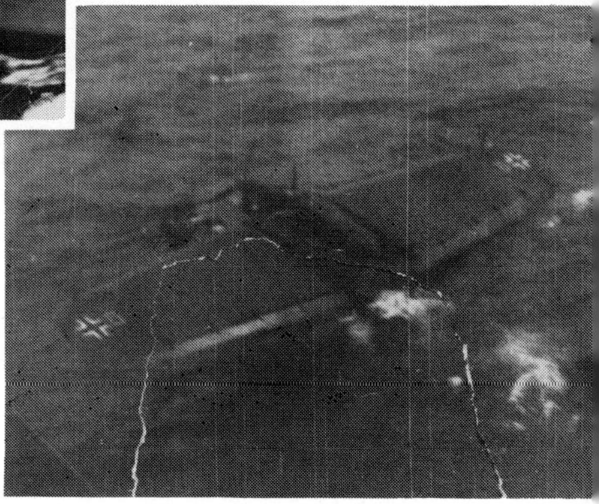

29 November 1939. This Dornier 18K flying boat had been shot down by a Battle Flight of No. 220 Squadron, Thornaby. We found it disabled on the water, brought along the Norwegian ship 'Bruse' and, when the crew had been picked up, sank it with machine gun fire. Our Station Commander told us we should have bombed the lot of them on the water!! Don't think he really meant it.

25 February 1940. Found these rafts with the sole survivors of a sunken ship. Brought a destroyer along to pick them up. Nice feeling to do someone a good turn!

R.A.F. PILOT FINDS MEN ON RAFT

WARSHIP RESCUES

The pilot of an R.A.F. Coastal Command aircraft on patrol early yesterday far out at sea saw in the half-light an object floating on the water. He came down to investigate and found a raft bearing six men. The sea was washing over them.

The men heard the 'plane, looked up and waved. The pilot circled round and then flew off to inform a destroyer and guide it to the raft Less than 50 minutes after they had been first seen the six men were safely on board the warship.

Norway but the weather was so awful that we packed it in and came home early. As a precaution against the day when I might have to ditch the aircraft in that cold North Sea I used to carry a small hip flask of ration rum that I'd scrounged from the Navy. At about the time that I reckoned the world had been fortunate enough to be graced by my presence 21 years earlier I produced my little bottle and offered it to Bill, who was doing the flying.

'My birthday, Bill, have a swig.'

'No thanks.'

'It's my 21st, Bill. Won't happen again. Just try a little one.'

'Thanks, no. Can't stand the stuff.'

Which was true, Bill wasn't a drinking man. I didn't really like rum myself but this was an occasion. I took a swig and wished myself a happy birthday.

'Many Happy Returns of the day, though,' said Bill. 'Is this course O.K.?' he continued suspiciously.

'Well, stick on three degrees to starboard if you feel like it, Bill. I'll go and twiddle the knobs in a minute or two but the wind *is* veering a bit, certainly.'

'Three degrees starboard it is,' said Bill, 'Steering two-three-oh degrees magnetic.'

'Two-three-oh magnetic,' I confirmed.

'This weather's getting a bit duff,' said Bill. 'Cloud's getting lower all the time and I can't see all that far. I'll have to stick below it. By the time we get to Peterhead even the birds will be walking.'

'Some coming of age,' I thought to myself. 'Hell of a good party! Hope we don't hit a hill.'

Early in the new year McLaren of A Flight had quite a spirited action with a Heinkel 111 which was presumably returning to its base after a reconnaissance of Scapa Flow. As the squadron Operations Record Book has it: 'On 10th January 1940 Flying Officer McLaren, with Pilot Officer Evans as second pilot, attacked a Heinkel 111. After two front gun attacks its undercarriage dropped half down and the rear guns were silenced. After all the front gun ammunition had been shot away he climbed above the Heinkel and dropped two 250 pound anti-submarine bombs on it from about 100 feet above but these both missed. They then attacked with several free gun beam and quarter attacks until the turret hydraulic system failed, making it impossible to train the guns, and the action had to be broken off. The Hudson expended 1,500 rounds of ammunition and was hit by eleven bullets from the Heinkel.'

I rather liked the air-to-air bombing touch, even though it may not have been cricket, so to speak.

Quite the most pleasant job that winter involved the picking up of survivors from a torpedoed ship. At about 1000 hours one cold February morning we spotted a large oil slick on the water. Floating in this was the usual messy debris that represented all that remained of a sunken ship and eventually we found a couple of life rafts with six or seven survivors on board. The sea wasn't very rough, fortunately, but they looked a very wet, cold and miserable bunch, tossing away in the oil-sodden sea surrounded by floating bits of wood, paint tins, buckets, cordage, etc., that was all that was left of their world now lying at the bottom of that cold ocean. We had passed a couple of our destroyers a few miles back so we dropped a smoke float to mark the position and went off and talked to the destroyers on the signal lamp. One of them peeled off and picked up the survivors and there was a nice glow of satisfaction inside me as I watched the men clamber up the side of the destroyer to warmth and relative safety before we turned north-eastward for Utsire to complete our outward patrol. It isn't all that often in war that you can do something constructive for a change.

A few weeks later it became known that the *Altmark* was trying to get back to Germany. In August '39 she had sailed out into the Atlantic to act as a supply vessel to the pocket battleships *Graf Spee* and *Deutschland.* After the sinking of the *Graf Spee* at the Battle of the River Plate the *Altmark* had disappeared into the South Atlantic but she was thought to be on her way home with 300 British Merchant Navy prisoners on board. On 15 February she had been reported off Bergen on a southerly course and the next day she was sighted by two of our Hudsons, and the cruiser *Arethusa* was able to intercept her. She was, however, escorted by two Norwegian destroyers who would not co-operate in allowing our ships to search her, and the three vessels eventually turned into Norwegian territorial waters and anchored in Josing Fjord. Captain Vian, in the destroyer *Cossack,* followed them in and demanded of the senior Norwegian officer that the prisoners be released to him. The Norwegian replied that the *Altmark* had been searched at Bergen the previous day, that she had no British prisoners on board and that she was unarmed. A naval Captain could hardly violate neutral waters on his own authority so the *Cossack* withdrew outside Norwegian territorial waters and a first-class international row brewed up. We were almost certain that the prisoners were on board and were not going to let the

Altmark get away without being searched. Wireless messages whistled to and fro and the next day Captain Vian took the *Cossack* back into the fjord and, boarding the *Altmark* in a style reminiscent of the days of Captain Horatio Hornblower, overcame the resistance of the *Altmark's* crew and rescued all 299 of the prisoners. The *Altmark* was also found to be armed with light and heavy machine-guns and the covering-up and lack of co-operation of the Norwegians gave much cause for comment. In those early months of the war, when almost every day a new set-back struck the unprepared British people, the cry of the *Cossack's* boarding party as they opened up the *Altmark's* holds to release the prisoners — 'The Navy's here' — was a welcome bit of good cheer that rang round the nation. It was good to know that Coastal Command's Hudsons had contributed in no small measure to it.

A further bit of good cheer that went very little further than a few miles from Leuchars was the torpedoing of a neutral ship somewhere in shallow water just off the Bell Rock lighthouse. The ship had been laden with a cargo of tins of ham and large kegs of butter destined, presumably, for America. As the tides broke her up the coastal currents carried quite a bit of this desirable cargo on to the beaches of our bombing range at Tentsmuir. The discovery was made by an armourer of the Range Party and I was early in on the deal as I was the squadron Armament Officer, and soon acquired a couple of tins of ham. Beachcombing rapidly became the station hobby as a constant stream of pedestrians, cyclists and the carriage trade went to and fro and spread out along the two-mile length of the beach to join the natural inhabitants in their search for food. At our approach clouds of little knots and dunlin rose from the water's edge and fled, wheeling and manoeuvring, and showing now their white underparts and now their darker backs. These must be the birds that Wentworth Day spoke of as looking 'like a thousand shillings shot from a gun,' and how right he was! Other waders looked, as they wheeled and disappeared and reappeared, like puffs of smoke blown from the barrels of a muzzle-loading gun on a windy day. As we encroached on their territory in our search for the elusive, half-buried tins of ham there was little difference, except in grace and speed and scale, between the sanderlings darting after their shrimps and sandhoppers and the blue-clad airmen calling a silent 'Tally ho' as they flung themselves on the tell-tale gleaming edge of a tin and excavated it from the sand. Throughout, the oyster catchers, unlike the friendly sanderlings, piped their trilling disapproval.

Some tins were easier to find, lying in the surf line, and well worth a wetting of your shoes to beat the next man to it, all thoughts of rank and dignity forgotten. The butter was another matter. Usually below the water line and weighing about a hundredweight it had to be a communal matter, a team of at least four being required to plunge into the water and heave it out of its sandy bed. Representing nine years' butter ration for one person, the kegs of butter were prizes indeed. Restricted as I was on one occasion to a bicycle borrowed from the armoury, I aimed humbly at the odd tin of ham and resented the smug looks on the faces of three C Flight pilots crammed with the driver and his bull terrier into an elderly Austin Seven as it lurched and bumped its way along the vile range track with a keg of butter in the back. The owner of the car suffered along with his overladen vehicle but the other three jabbed their bifurcated digits skywards as though to say 'Improve on that one, if you can, Dopey.'

God is ever on the side of the big battalions of course, but, give those chaps their due, they were pretty generous in the way they lashed out their butter. As a matter of fact a hundredweight of butter was something of a liability; it was far too much, even for four to share, and their generosity reached embarrasing proportions as they finally tried to get rid of pounds of the slippery stuff. On our patrols we carried sandwiches in which quarter-inch thick slices of ham squelched in a sea of butter. We openly pitied Bomber Command flying their lumbering Whitleys on the asinine, but dangerous, leaflet raids over the Third Reich.

'I'll bet they only have bully-beef sandwiches on those trips, poor buggers,' opined someone.

'Serves them right for not going to sea,' said another, forgetting them instantly.

It was rumoured that female moral standards had deteriorated somewhat as a result of the bonanza, the ham and butter being the 1940 equivalent of the nylon stockings brought in later in the war by the Merchant Navy and Transport Command crews. After all, the ladies had to keep up their strength.

It couldn't last, of course. The Station Commander received a telephone call one day from a gentleman whose very voice implied that you can do anything you like on this earth so long as you don't enjoy yourself while doing it. He was the local Excise Officer. 'I've heerd tell, Group Captain, of infringements of the Customs and Excise Act, 1789, Schedule D, as amended. I've had information laid to the effect that your airmen are removing His

Majesty's property from the foreshore of the bombing range at Tentsmuir in the form of ham and butter.'

'Good heavens,' said the Group Captain. 'I'll put a stop to it immediately.'

'Thank you, sir, but there is the matter of the goods already stolen.'

'*Alleged* to have been stolen, I take it you mean,' said the Groupie.

The Excise man swallowed his pride and agreed. But continued, 'I should like permission to search the station, sir.'

'Quite impossible,' said the Groupie. 'This is an operational station of a nation at war; the place is full of secrets (hundredweights of the stuff, he muttered to himself). I couldn't possibly let you in.'

'I am afraid, Group Captain, that you have no powers to prevent me. I am empowered to search all premises above the high water mark. My team will be there at 1400 hours today.

'You may well be here at 1400 hours today, Mr McPherson, but you will not get past the guardroom. We have mounted an operation of the utmost importance and I cannot compromise its security in any way at all. No stranger will set foot in this camp until 0800 hours tomorrow.'

'At 0800 hours tomorrow, then, Group Captain.'

The Tannoy public address system came to life. 'This is the Station Commander speaking. A team of Excise Officers will be visiting the station at 0800 hours tomorrow searching for items allegedly removed from Tentsmuir ranges. I am quite satisfied that no such items will be found, but Squadron Commanders are to make their own arrangements to deal with this as they think fit. Disciplinary action may be taken against anyone whom the Excise authorities find to be in possession of any of these alleged items.' He put the microphone down.

'And, Chota,' he said to the Adjutant, 'ring my wife and tell her to take all our stuff over to her sister's place until this lot blows over. Just in case they search the married quarters.'

In 233 Squadron it was felt that it would be better to give the goons something to bite on so the better-heeled were persuaded to hide the odd tin of ham in places where they would probably be found and lots were drawn to boost the caches a bit. The dispersal of the loot was fairly easy to organise, the bomb dump being a favourite place on account of the number of areas to which people were forbidden entry on safety grounds. Most aircrew put them in our 15 cwt Bedfords and moved these from dispersal point to dispersal point as necessary. Gun turret ammunition tanks took a tin of ham when 100 rounds of ammo was removed from the belt, the remaining 400 rounds folding over nicely so as just to fill the tank — though one unfortunate armourer lost his lot when a cunning gunner found the loot during a check on his loads and took off a hundred rounds short on one gun rather than forgo the bounty. Codes and cypher people just popped them in their safes. Butter owners had the most difficult time disposing of their more bulky kegs and, in most cases, had to fork out a proportion of the keg to those in charge of places that could accommodate the stuff, such as bomb dumps and paint stores. The whole episode was a fillip to station morale, not only gastronomically but also because of the defeat of the forces of law and order. When the goons left the station they did so with only about seven tins of ham and with no butter at all.

Returning from Norway on one patrol we sighted an aircraft many miles away and found one of our elderly London flying boats circling a Tribal class destroyer. The Londons, and the similar Stranraers, were twin-engined biplane flying boats of some antiquity and were all that could be spared for this northern area of operations as the Wick and Aberdeen squadrons had still not yet converted to Hudsons. These old boats were slow but could stay airborne for many hours and they did useful patrol work. We talked to the destroyer with our Aldis lamp and learned that she was the famous *Cossack* of *Altmark* fame a month or so before. She was on to a U-boat and asked for our help. We were a bit short of fuel but we throttled back to conserve our remaining stock and joined the London in her stately progress. After a while the London sailed down to sea level and dropped a bomb which went off with a good shower of spray but I couldn't see any target so stayed where I was. The *Cossack* heeled over in a steep turn and swept in to drop a depth-charge that made a mighty shivering in the sea before the spray came up, but I didn't see any result from either attack and eventually had to leave due to fuel shortage. We landed at Leuchars after 8 hours and 10 minutes, the longest I've ever stretched a patrol to, coming straight in on the runway without any preliminary, fuel-burning circuit. The ground crew were surprised to see us; they'd already added us to the list of those who had failed to return.

On 9 April we were nearing the Norwegian coast when I noticed that one of the four retaining bolts on the emergency exit hatch above my head was loose so I made a note on my knee pad to tell the rigger when we landed. A little later we sighted a

Heinkel 115 twin-engined floatplane so closed in to attack it with the front guns. I called up the gunner on the intercom. 'It'll probably be all front gun work at first, Valentine, but try and get a shot off from the turret if the opportunity arises.'

As we came up astern of him his rear gunner opened fire and his tracer smoke reached out at us, but he'd started firing a bit on the early side and I closed the range before getting to work with the front Brownings. When, at last, the range came down to about 200 yards I pressed the gun button and the clattering of the Brownings and the smell of cordite fumes were a comfort after the wait to get in closer.

Once the shooting match starts you are, as pilot, aware of little else beside the target and the gunsight. The aircraft becomes merely an extension of your mind as you operate throttles, control column and rudder bar to keep the target at the correct deflection in the sight, aiming not at, but ahead of it. It's not all that easy to hit an aircraft, even with two guns firing forty shots a second, as the whole thing has to be done on your estimation of speeds and angles; and the target makes your job as difficult as possible, of course, by twisting and turning and altering speed so as to throw you out in those estimations. What the gunnery manuals forgot to mention, of course, was that return fire from the target could also affect one's estimations if one was of nervous disposition. So it takes a lot of ammunition to shoot down an aircraft, even by fighter pilots whose sole job it is. To us reconnaissance pilots shooting was only a sideline, occasionally indulged in if we met our opposite numbers of the Luftwaffe on *their* recce sorties. The aircraft of our reconnaissance world weighed three times as much as a fighter, were 100 mph slower and had only one or two guns firing forward, as compared with a fighter's eight. We were not, therefore, aces of air combat hailed regularly in the Press for our knightly prowess, but we did our best. I never, to my knowledge, shot down an enemy aircraft. On the other hand neither did any of them shoot *me* down, and as the majority of aircraft which later shot at me were Messerschmitt 109s and 110s — the professional fighter boys — they had far less excuse for the poor results. It was a good thing that the taxpayer never got to know just how much ammunition it took to shoot down an aircraft or he'd have asked for his money back[1].

The fight with the 115 was lasting quite a time and was taking place between two sheets of stratus cloud quite widely separated in height. I tried to head off the 115 if he made for either of these

[1] See Appendix 1 for technical information on Deflection Shooting.

cloud layers but it looked as though one of his efforts to climb into the layer on top was having a certain amount of success so I rammed the throttles to the gate and went after him. As I thumbed the gun button for the next burst there was an almighty bang and a tremendous suction as the already weakened emergency hatch bolts above my head gave way and the hatch flew out. The roaring of the slipstream and the crackling of the gunfire from the 115 became immediately apparent but were swamped as the immense draught flowing out of the roof brought every bit of dust, grit and grass seed from the cabin floor swirling round the cockpit and into our eyes and mouths. I was half blinded and, as I screwed up my eyes, it became evident that the slipstream noise seemed incredibly loud for a climbing aircraft and that the controls had become very stiff. I opened my eyes and stole a look at the airspeed indicator, then immediately wished I hadn't. Absorbed in my gunsight I had failed to realise the the Heinkel wasn't climbing for the cloud layer above but was diving fast for the layer below. At over 300 knots indicated we were well above our maximum permitted speed as we screamed downhill after the Heinkel and I chopped the throttles back quick. We were overhauling him fast and the highly audible crack-crack-crack of his bullets going past was followed by the more muted pop-pop-popping of his gun until, at last, there was no more return fire. Either I'd hit his rear gunner or he was out of ammunition, but I imagine that they thought he had done rather well to shoot such a large lump out of us. We ding-donged for about half an hour all told before he finally evaded us in cloud, though he now appeared to be losing petrol from one tank when he turned.

We took stock. It was devilishly cold and noisy in the roofless cockpit, especially as the heating system of the Hudson was so good that the pilot flew in shirt sleeves as often as not, and it was one of my 'often' days. I had heard at least one shot go through the cabin but nothing untoward showed on the instrument panel so the engines were probably O.K. and we gathered ourselves to complete the patrol. I strapped my helmet tightly in place and we continued on our course for Norway, sorted out our position and set off back for Leuchars. Bill, who was navigating, was feeling a bit airsick after the combat but we struggled with the charts in the windy cockpit and sorted out a course for home. The rest of the patrol was uneventful and we made a reasonable landfall only a few miles from our intended track. April is not, however, the best month for tanking along with your sunshine roof open and we were frozen to the marrow by the time we landed.

Full of ourselves, and bursting to tell the world of our first air combat, we strode into the Ops Room to find that we had been well beaten to the post. We joined on at the end of a queue of Heinkel 115-fighters waiting to tell the Intelligence Officer their life stories. In 233 Squadron alone Rhein and Sgt Glover had shot at *two* of them, Williams and Ensor had had a go at one, as also had Vercoe and Sgt Piercey. At the other end of the room 224 Squadron were being equally voluble. I chatted up the bloke ahead of me in the queue. 'Trade's brisk this morning, Tubby.'

'Yes, we had a hell of a fight with a Heinkel 115 this morning. Ever seen one? Bloody great twin-engined floatplane all covered in swastikas and things.'

'Yes, Tubby, we had one, too.'

'You see, we saw him miles away and popped into cloud for our approach then Willie just stuffed his nose down and went at him flat out. Hell of a fight!'

'Yes Tubby we had one too.'

'What's that Dopey? Oh, yes, I was saying. Real ding-dong it was. Bullets flying all over the shop. You should have been there, Dopey.'

'I was.'

'Then, about half-way through, the tracer *really* came at us. Ever seen tracer smoke, Dopey? Puts you off a bit. You know that every bit of smoke has got a hard centre. Didn't affect Willie, though. He still went after him. And the smell of cordite fumes! Jeeze!'

'We lost our emergency exit, Tubby. We could *hear* the shots going past then.'

'That Rheinmetal free gun of the Luftwaffe's certainly dishes out the shit,' said Tubby. 'Fires nearly as fast as a bloody Browning. Thank your lucky stars you've never been on the receiving end, Dopey.'

I gave up. 'Yes, Tubby. But what's all the activity this morning? Just look at this mob.'

I waved at the assembled aircrew. Everywhere arms were raised and hands flew gracefully through the air representing Hudsons attacking Heinkels. The hands swept down in quarter attacks, slid astern and continued to pump in the bullets. The left hands (Heinkel hands) slid away in evasion and the right (Hudson) hands followed remorselessly. A right hand would rise and give the left hand a devastating burst into the belly from below. You could nearly *see* the destruction in that Heinkel fuselage. The left hand would move downwards into a desperate dive to sea level, a move completely defeated by the right hand which, with consummate skill, dived even faster (you could nearly *feel* that negative G) to come up in yet another rising quarter attack.

'Look, Tubby, we must have shot down half the bloody Luftwaffe this morning. How many confirmed?'

'Er, actually, I don't think we've shot down any, Dopey.'

It looked as though they were all as bad a shot as I was. 'But what's up, Tubby? We've all been bloody busy.'

'Christ, haven't you heard? Germany invaded Norway this morning.'

'So that's what it's all about. Bit rough on the Norwegians, isn't it?' It was *very* rough on the Norwegians. It was also going to be reasonably rough on us, though we didn't know it yet.

Chapter 3

The North Sea, which had been gradually emptying of merchant vessels, now started to become busy with naval movements. The next day we escorted the six-inch-gun cruiser *Aurora* into the Pentland Firth and the day after we flew over Norwegian territory for the first time looking for German ships in the coastal fjords. Luftwaffe activity was maintained and McLaren, who was now commanding A Flight, had a fight with a Dornier 18K flying boat during which his second pilot, the gentle Evans, was fatally shot and died on the way home. McLaren himself was killed the next day when the squadron was out looking for the battle cruiser *Scharnhorst.* A sighting report came over the radio that the *Scharnhorst* and another ship, probably the cruiser *Hipper,* had been found and all available aircraft were ordered to close on the ships and attack them. McLaren and Yorke, a New Zealander, did not return from this operation. Bill and I were so far south when the message came through that we hadn't the fuel to reach the ships and we continued our course home.

As the Norwegian Expeditionary Force crossed the North Sea on the forlorn and familiar too-little-and-too-late effort that was all we could manage in the first years of the war, the demand on us for escorts grew greatly and interference by the Luftwaffe became acute as the Germans had occupied all the aerodromes in Norway and had complete air superiority. Norway was to be the first of many harsh lessons to be rammed home; no army or navy could cope against overwhelming local air superiority. From Norway and the Battle of France, right up to the sinking of the *Prince of Wales* and the *Repulse* two years later by the Japanese, it was to be proved over and over again that it was quite impossible to operate unless you had reasonable control of the air. On our patrols we were now meeting not only the slow reconnaissance aircraft such as the Dornier 18K and Heinkel 115 but also the Luftwaffe's best fighter, the Messerschmitt 109. The 109 was 100 mph faster than we were and carried the formidable armament of a 20 mm cannon and four rifle-calibre machine-guns. It was also operating on its own doorstep so that it stood a good chance of getting back to base if damaged or, at least, of allowing its pilot to bale out over land. If we survived an action we had anything up to 450 miles of sea over which to bring back a possibly damaged aircraft; and flying as we did on south-westerly courses, a southerly error in navigation could mean missing the coast near Leuchars and not making a landfall until the coast of Berwickshire turned up at an appreciable distance later, which could use up a fair amount of petrol. From Stavanger also operated the bombers which attacked the Army and Navy units further north at Aandalsnes and it was decided that HMS *Suffolk* (about whom circulated one of the ruder 'knock-knock' jokes of that period)[1] would bombard Stavanger aerodrome at first light on 17 April. *Suffolk* was a 10,000-ton cruiser carrying a main armament of eight eight-inch guns, each firing a 250 lb shell, so she could put down a pretty effective barrage. It was, of course, a very bold decision to use her (we were still learning the art of war the hard way) as this area of sea was normally left to our submarines and to us in Coastal Command.

The day before, there was a long planning session in the Operations room attended by naval officers from Rosyth. Bill and I, and Laurie Ewing and his second pilot were also present. The Luftwaffe were going to react strongly to the stirring up of their wasps' nest and it was accepted that it was going to be a vigorously defended action on their part. *Suffolk* was to catapult off one of her Walrus amphibians to spot for the gunfire. If there was any difficulty ('i.e., when the poor sod is shot down,' muttered Bill) a second Walrus would be shot off and, if that had similar difficulty, Bill and I were to take over, Laurie Ewing substituting for us when we'd been given the treatment.

'If you ask me,' said Bill . . .

'I wasn't,' I said.

'That coastline,' continued Bill unnecessarily (I'd got the message), 'is going to be knee-deep in wrecked Steam Chickens[2] and Hudsons.'

[1]HMS *Suffolk* had been on the West Indies station for about three years and was then brought back to the UK for a welcome Home Fleet commission. She had no sooner got back than trouble blew up in the Far East and she was sent off immediately to the China station, a highly unpopular move with the crew, who were just getting to know their families all over again. As she went across the bay of Biscay she passed a destroyer homeward bound from Gibraltar.

'Knock, knock,' signalled *Suffolk*.

'Who's there,' obediently replied the destroyer.

'*Suffolk*.'

'*Suffolk* who?'

'Suffolking long way to China.'

[2]Steam Chicken — the Walrus aircraft, also known as a "Shagbat".

'Did you say something, Pilot Officer Tacon?' queried the Intelligence Officer who was briefing us.

'No, Sir, I was just agreeing that it was a good idea to have back-up aircraft.'

We were to carry a bomb load of the new 25 lb incendiary bombs, which we were to drop on some likely spot on the aerodrome to try to start a fire on which the *Suffolk* could lay her guns. We would also drop a flare at the same time over the centre of the aerodrome. I was to have a Lieutenant Commander as my naval observer and a naval telegraphist/air gunner to operate the wireless set while on the shoot. Our own wireless operator, Corporal Purves would be on the set for the rest of the time and Leading Aircraftman McAdie was our gunner, making a crew of six all told.

On the 17th we took off at 0115 hours and circled round with our navigation lights on, waiting for Laurie Ewing to join us. After a while the runway floodlights went out but we could see no sign of Laurie's aircraft and, as rigid wireless silence was imposed until the shoot started, we had to set off without him or we'd be late for the rendezvous. I hoped he would catch up with us later. Laurie Ewing, a New Zealander like Bill Tacon, was a tough egg and it would be nice to have him along. As it turned out he didn't make it; he had had an electrical failure just after take-off and had to turn back. It would have been a serious fault as Laurie wouldn't let a small thing like the odd light not working keep him out of the air.

We switched off our navigation lights and set off for Stavanger. Just before rendezvous time we passed over a barely discernible naval ship a thousand feet beneath us on a course just south of east. It was bound to be *Suffolk* on her way from Scapa Flow but we couldn't communicate until rendezvous time. In the cold light of dawn the grey ship on the heaving grey waters was almost invisible, apart from the churning wake left by her rapid progress through the water. She must have been doing 25 knots. Within fifteen seconds she had vanished from our ken as though she'd never been there but it looked as though we were both fairly well on track and should meet up at the rendezvous all right.

We made our landfall and got into position just on the coastline at about 3,000 feet, which gave us a good view of the aerodrome and of *Suffolk* a couple of miles out to sea. As we ran in some anti-aircraft hate came up at us but we dropped our incendiaries in one lump and carried on to release a flare just to the upwind side of the aerodrome before returning to the spotting line. The radio was now the responsibility of the Navy and I just drove up and down so as to give the observer a good view of the target. I saw the first four gouts of ruddy flame as the *Suffolk* fired one gun from each turret but couldn't see any result on the aerodrome. After a few more salvoes a fire seemed to start in the seaplane anchorage some distance away but I was now well occupied with an anti-aircraft look-out and the naval people seemed quite busy at their work so I left them to get on with it as I flew the short legs up and down the target area. I was expecting a sharp reaction from the Luftwaffe in the shape of a horde of 109s and was hoping that Laurie Ewing would soon appear to give a bit of cross-fire support if we were jumped.

After a while it looked as though we were going to get some assistance after all. The gunner came up on the intercom 'Aircraft coming up astern, sir. Looks like a Mark IV Blenheim.'

Good, a fighter Blenheim with five front guns. Nice of them to send it, though he wouldn't have much fuel available for a dogfight after the long trip he'd had getting over here. 'O.K. McAdie, let me know when he comes up with us.'

Tracer smoke streaked by six feet underneath me and spiralled ahead. I slammed the throttles fully open and had started a steep left-hand turn when McAdie's belated 'He's opened fire. He looks like a Junkers 88,' came over the intercom, together with the rattle of his own guns and the tinkling of the links and empty cases as they fell into the empties bag. An embarassing, but perhaps forgivable, mistake. In the still-poor light before sunrise the frontal views of the two aircraft were very similar. Under normal circumstances I'd have turned immediately any aircraft was sighted so as to investigate and be either in a reasonable position to attack or a difficult one from which to be attacked, depending on what the opposition was. Concentrating, as we were, on giving the spotting officer as good a view as possible I'd allowed the 88 to get right up my jumper. If I'd turned towards him in time I could have had an initial belt at him as we shot at each other head-on before starting the formalised waltzing and jockeying around of trying to get on each other's tail. We were probably a fairly evenly matched pair and, had the action started in this way, I would have stood as good a chance of doing him a lot of damage as he to me. I'd notched up my first thousand hours as a pilot a fortnight before and now knew the Hudson well and was confident of putting up a reasonably good show with it. However, I was not to have the opportunity. He was on our tail and nothing I could do would shake him off it. I didn't fire my front guns once but McAdie in the turret was as busy as he could be. All thought of the spotting duty vanished as we twisted and heaved and turned to give the 88 as big a deflection shot as possible. If he came in from the left I could see him as he closed in and I gave the stick an extra hard yank back as I saw his gun flashes. If he came in from the right a combination of advice from the gunner and from Bill Tacon enabled me to do what seemed best at the time. I felt a great deal of sympathy for the naval officer as he had no seat to sit on and had to get out of the way at intervals as Bill dashed up and down the aircraft from the observation dome in the cabin to me in the cockpit with advice on avoiding action. With the considerable G forces operating as we turned and twisted he was flung all over the place, clinging on as best he could.

After about the statutory half hour that our combats seemed to last I saw, as I looked at the 88 over my shoulder, a good burst from McAdie go in the region of his port engine. Either because of that, or because he'd shot off all his ammunition, he then broke away and vanished. 'If you're going to Stavanger, mate,' I thought, 'you're in for a hectic landing. I'd try Kristiansand if I were you.' We did the usual stock-taking as to the state of the aircraft. I'd heard about five bullets go through the fuselage but they all seemed to be in innocuous places and the engines sounded and looked as good as ever. We found ourselves about 20 miles south of Stavanger so set off to rejoin *Suffolk*.

We found her still at it and, a short time after, I noticed that the midships four-inch guns had also started firing, which was a bit odd as they couldn't possibly have ranged as far as the aerodrome, where impressive gouts of earth shot up into the air from time to time as the eight-inch bricks landed. They normally only used the four-inch stuff as anti-aircraft. 'Christ, that rings a bell,' I thought and had a quick look around. The air was dotted with the puffs of exploded anti-aircraft shells and two more went off as I looked. We weren't the only ones bad at aircraft recognition that morning. Not for the first time in this campaign (or throughout the war for that matter) the Navy was shooting first and would ask the questions after. I didn't blame them; it would take them a long time to get home from this shoot and better to be sure than sorry. I could afford this generosity of spirit as, apart from my natural nobility of character, I was comforted by the knowledge of the hideous inaccuracy of heavy ack-ack fire from ships. In my view it was a sheer waste of time carting heavy anti-aircraft guns around on a ship. If they'd used the weight and space on 40 and 20 mm automatic guns then the aviator would have far more sleepless nights just thinking about them. It was the machine-guns and light automatics that knocked aircraft out of the sky.

We fired off the current recognition signal with the Very pistol, gave them a short, blasphemous message on the wireless and took up our spotting line again, now keeping an extra good look-out for the fighters which must surely arrive any minute. The naval chap seemed to be busy, the telegraphist was tapping away at his morse key and the rest of the task passed off, to our surprise, quite peacefully. *Suffolk* fired off her last salvo and turned away westward at full speed as we swung south-westward for Leuchars.

We had an uneventful trip home but I felt quite a glow of satisfaction with a job done as well as we could in the circumstances. During the action I had quite forgotten about the Walruses which were to be shot off the *Suffolk's* catapult to do the initial spot and hoped that they had got on well; I didn't envy them. We arrived back home in nice time for breakfast but were a bit disconcerted when the ground crew waving us in to the tarmac suddenly took to their heels and vanished. 'What a hell of a fine welcome,' I thought, 'And, welcome' aside, they're an undisciplined rabble. They'll get the rough end of my tongue when I get out. I'll have the lot of them on a charge.' And then the reason for their behaviour became apparent as a maroon-red object rolled ahead of us on the tarmac. It was one of the new-fangled 25 lb incendiary bombs which we had carried: It had evidently hung up on the rack when we'd dropped them at Stavanger and the extra G forces imposed during the fight with the Junkers 88 had dragged it off the rack to roll loosely around the belly in a fully-armed condition for the rest of the trip. We were lucky it hadn't gone off in the bomb-bay. As I had taxied in I had opened the bomb doors and the bomb had dropped out. One look at the sinister object was enough for the ground crew and they took to their heels. Anyway there it was, in my court, so to speak. I shut the Hudson down rapidly and streaked out of the cockpit. A glance at the bomb told my experienced eye that it was quite safe and I hailed the first face peering round the corner of the hangar with the reassurance that all was well and that the attention of him and his mates would be appreciated within the next second-and-a-half to help us unload the aircraft. I apologised when they had reassembled and some menial was deputed to carry the thing away to the bomb dump.

17 February 1940. The German prison ship 'Altmark' in Josing Fiord. She had been supply ship to the pocket battleship 'Graf von Spee', which had been sunk after the Battle of the River Plate in December 1939. 'Altmark' had 299 British merchant seamen prisoners on board and they were liberated by Captain Philip Vian in the destroyer 'Cossack', in a spirited Hornblower-type engagement. (I.W.M.)

Destroyer 'Cossack'. (I.W.M.)

One of our landfalls in Norway – Lister. April 1940, when searching for 'Scharnhorst' (mentioned in DFC citation, later) Lister fiord in background. German ships regularly hid in the steep-sided fiords, which made aircraft attack extremely difficult.

Type V11C U-boat under attack, with depth charges and machine guns. (I.W.M.)

16 March 1940. A 'London' flying boat of the type that was helping HMS 'Cossack' hunt a U-Boat. Note long-range petrol tank between the wings, the 250 lb. bomb under the wing and the three open gun positions – in the nose, amidships and in the tail. (I.W.M.)

9 April 1940, the day Germany invaded Norway. My first aerial combat with one of these Heinkel 115 floatplanes. We probably damaged one of his petrol tanks but we lost the roof escape hatch and had a very cold trip home. (I.W.M.)

'Scharnhorst'. 26,000 tons of hell on earth. Apart from her main and secondary armaments of 9 x 11" and 12 x 5.9" guns she had 14 x 4.1" and 16 x 37 mm anti-aircraft guns. The East coast Hudson squadrons spent quite a lot of time searching for, and attacking her. (I.W.M.)

'Suffolk'. 10,000 ton County Class cruiser. 8 x 8" and 6 x 4" guns. Up to three Walrus aircraft. On 17 April 1940 we spotted for the fall of shot while she fired 202 x 8" shells, each weighing 250 lbs., into Stavanger aerodrome. She was seriously damaged by dive bombers shortly afterwards and had to be beached at Scapa Flow on her return in order to prevent her from sinking. The large square structure behind the funnels is the aircraft hangar. Running across the ship between these can be seen the aircraft catapult. (I.W.M.)

When we de-briefed in the operations room it looked as though it had been a well-executed operation and there were congratulations all round at the successful inter-services co-operation. (We did hear later, though, that *Suffolk* had been bombed on the way home and had suffered some damage.) We went off to the Mess for the very welcome aircrew breakfast of bacon and egg to tell our story to the fire-eating Laurie Ewing, who had missed the trip through the unserviceability of his aircraft. While we had returned unscathed, we had set off fully expecting a packet of trouble; we weren't daft. If they were laying on four spotting aircraft it was because they thought they'd need them, but some stroke of luck had come our way and the trip didn't end up in the expected slaughter of the innocents. The navigation had gone quite well and we'd rendezvoued dead on time. I'd been a bit careless in letting that Junkers 88 get up my jumper but we'd survived and I think we sent him away, if not with a flea in his ear with, perhaps, a load of bullets in his port engine. It hadn't been a bad sort of day. The bacon and eggs were great, the coffee supportable, the toast wonderful and the Mess still had its hoard of illegal butter. There were worse occupations in life than that of a Coastal Command pilot, which makes it all the more difficult to write what follows.

You would expect a person of my (present) age to have few, if any, illusions — they are, after all, the prerogatives of youth. But I never had any doubts about the fact that we did a reasonably good job spotting for *Suffolk* that April day in 1940; and I thought so, if I ever *did* think about it, for 40 years. In the interests of the accuracy of this book I had done some research in the Public Records Office looking up my squadron's Operation Record Book and so on. Unfortunately I let my zeal run away with me and I thought I'd add the final touch of realism by approaching the Naval Historical Branch to get the web-footed angle on the operation. Their courteous letter informed me:

(i) In the absence of any German fighter aircraft at Stavanger aerodrome it had been decided to use the Walrus aircraft.

(ii) *Suffolk* had catapulted off both her Walri and, happily both aircraft had managed to get home, one to Scapa Flow and the other to Aberdeen.

(iii) Wasn't it a pity that none of the three aircraft had managed to establish radio communication with the ship, which had had to conduct an unobserved shoot?

If I'd known about (i) I would have been far happier stooging up and down Stavanger like a fat goose waiting to be plucked by the first Messerschmitt 109 that appeared. Why on earth hadn't anyone told us at the time?

I was very glad to hear about (ii), though how on earth those Walri carried enough fuel for that return trip I just don't know. They must have rowed the aircraft the last few miles.

(iii), on the other hand, was an absolute facer. Neither of the naval crew in our Hudson had mentioned the failure of radio communication to me either in the air or at de-briefing. It made the whole operation such an absolute fiasco, especially as *Suffolk* had been bombed on the way home. In chastened mood I wrote back to the Naval Historical Branch. Would they be kind enough to elaborate on their previous letter? They were, unfortunately, kind enough and their second letter was far, far worse. I wished that I'd let well, or ill, alone.

The mistakes, omissions, lack of information, failure to impart known information, unfortunate or plain daft choices all combined to make 'Operation Duck' (we hadn't even known its code-name but, in retrospect, I feel that Donald Duck must have had a hand in it) an expensive and frustrating affair. The biggest single error was the choosing of a radio frequency which, in the stormy post-mortem conducted afterwards, of which I was unaware, was stated 'to have been found by Hudson aircraft to be unreliable at night and dawn and which therefore had been discarded as a night frequency.' On the day of the shoot *Suffolk* read one spotting correction from her No. 1 Walrus and one from us and nothing else. The No. 2 Walrus, which was catapulted off later, at about the time we returned from our fight with the Junkers 88, reverted to visual signalling with her Aldis lamp.

The opening round was to set the pattern for the whole affair. Apparently the anti-aircraft fire which the aerodrome defences shot off at us as we did our incendiary run-in was enough to prevent the *Suffolk* from identifying our flare — to them it appeared to be all part of the general Guy Fawkes performance which you could expect when you fly over a chap's aerodrome at four in the morning and drop bombs on him. Which we found odd as the flak wasn't all that bad and was an integral part of one's contract of employment, so to speak. But to the *Suffolk,* ten thousand yards out to sea, what seemed to us to be a brilliantly-burning magnesium flare was just one in a number of pyrotechnics lighting up the eastern sky and, as radio contact proved non-existent, she did her shoot under the greatest difficulties, and with a fair degree of inaccuracy, I would imagine.

In all, *Suffolk* fired 202 eight-inch rounds, the equivalent of the bomb load that fifty Hudsons could carry. What was to prove expensive was that during the night of 16 April, on her way out from Scapa Flow, the *Suffolk* had been ordered to sweep northwards after the bombardment to intercept some German destroyers so, after the shoot, she withdrew westwards away from the dangers of land contact, for 30 miles before turning northwards at 25 knots to close on the destroyers. The fighter escort that Coastal Command had laid on expected to find *Suffolk* sailing northward close in-shore and nobody told them that she'd be a further 30 miles out to sea so they made no contact and *Suffolk* was left without an escort. Throughout the day, from 0825 to 1512 hours she was attacked by 33 aircraft which dropped 88 bombs, one of which scored a direct hit. At 1037 hours a dive-bomber had got home with a very heavy bomb which caused severe damage, putting both after-turrets out of action, reducing her speed to 18 knots and causing flooding to the extent of 1,500 tons of water in 20 minutes. Near-misses continued to shake up the ship and caused further extensive flooding and, by 1305 hours, both of her steering motors went out of action, though these were repaired 20 minutes later. The first friendly aircraft arrived at 1415 hours and, by 1430 hours, nine of them were in company, probably a mixed bag of Coastal Command Blenheims and Hudsons together with some Fleet Air Arm Skuas from Hatston. These did not, however, prevent further, and extremely accurate, attacks upon the ship, which was badly shaken by the near-misses. By 1620 hours the two huge battle cruisers *Renown* and *Repulse* had arrived to escort the struggling *Suffolk* but it was to be the next day, the 18th, before she crawled into Scapa Flow with her quarter-deck awash and her steering gear finally broken down so that she could only steer on her propellers. She was in such a state that she had to be beached immediately to prevent her from sinking. After temporary repairs, she was sent to the Clyde for permanent repairs on 5 May.

When one reads about this sort of thing one wonders how the war was ever won. The simple answer is that the other side do exactly similar things, of course, and, in the case of the Nazi dictatorship, far worse inefficiencies were heaped from above by Hitler's personal intervention on to their military planners' existing mistakes. On the credit side, actions that seemed of no consequence at the time were found later to have had bonuses of vast significance. You can't practise a war in peacetime; you have to fight it to find out how to do it. But it was a great disappointment to find out that I had been playing a lead part in one of the cock-ups.

At the time, however, we were flushed with a feeling of success; it was nice to have put up such a good show for the Navy. Two days later we were sent to do a recce of Bjorne Fjord as the Germans were moving a lot of stuff along the innumerable waterways sheltered from the sea by the offshore islands, which made it almost impossible for the Navy to interfere with them.

'While you're in that part of the world,' said the Ops Room Controller, 'have a good look at Haugesund harbour. We've had reports of German light naval units using the place and some of our chaps have been fired on by a machine-gun located somewhere on the waterfront. Get some good photographs if you can.'

We did our recce of Bjorne Fjord. Hunting up and down the fjords could be quite pleasant flying. Some of the fjord systems, such as Hardanger and Sogne Fjords, were very extensive and you could fly for hours and still not cover them all. Sometimes, as we had a habit of flying as low as possible to avoid any radar, we would end up towards the top end of a very steep-sided fjord and have to do a really tight turn to get out of it, with the belly of the Hudson flitting around not many feet from the rocky sides. Some of the scenery was quite fantastic, jagged ranges of snow-covered mountains vanishing into the interior for miles, and some of the sunrises were breathtaking as the rays of the rising sun struck numerous mountain-tops at different angles, each with its topping of pink icing. As a pilot, if you feel like playing and have the time, and it looks as though the Hun isn't about, you can get some extra sunrises by diving steeply as soon as the sun is up so that it vanishes behind the mountains. In a few seconds, and all for free, you get your little treat all over again, though with inevitable and delightful differences this time because the angles of the sun's rays have altered, so the colours alter with it.

As we flew towards Haugesund Bill came up from the nose with the chart and laid it on my knees. 'If we run northwards between Karmoy Island, here, and the waterfront we can get a really good look at Haugesund so long as you come fairly low.' he said. 'If we're to sniff out that gunpost we'll *have* to be low. I can stick the hand-held camera out of the side window and get some really good shots of the quayside, which is a pretty long one. Keep about 300 yards off-shore and I'll get some good overlaps on the photos.

'O.K. Bill. I'll do the run at about 50 feet but I'll have to rise a bit as we approach Risoy Island to clear the buildings and that's where a lot of the ships are moored.'

Bill opened the side window and got hold of the hand-held camera. As I lost height and skated along the water he started cranking away at his photos as soon as the first waterfront buildings came up to the south of the main port. I concentrated on the job of keeping straight and level as we belted along the smooth water of the sheltered harbour. After a short while I heard the crack-crack-crack of machine-gun bullets going past the open window. 'Can you spot that bloody gun?' I yelled to Bill.

'No. I'm busy. Keep her going as she is. I'm getting some good shots.'

'You'll be getting some good shots up your jumper if you don't watch out,' I muttered to myself. I turned right a fraction to keep the same distance from the waterfront to try and maintain the scale of the camera shots and, at the same time, the machine-gun fire became noticeably more accurate. The crackling suddenly became much louder, each bullet cracking past with a flat, staccato wallop as it sped on its supersonic way so very close to us. Whoever that gunner was he had the deflection worked out to perfection as shots were now going through the fuselage with the customary splintery crash and I felt it was high time to give him best. Just ahead of us a large arched bridge curved over the hundred-yard-wide strip of water separating the mainland from Risoy Island, towards which we were heading. The sloping ground of the mainland and the buildings on Risoy Island made of the strip of water a steep-sided gulley in which I felt I could get away from the accursed gun, the waterfront here taking a turn to the right, which would be to our advantage. Once I got into that gulley we'd be out of the field of fire.

'I'm going under the bridge, Bill,' I yelled and did a quick right-left shimmy to get lined up to shoot underneath. The area was cluttered with fishing boats and their masts which didn't leave me all that much room and made the approach and exit a bit untidy-looking. I didn't know whether or not Bill was still winding away with the camera but he was quite capable of it; he wasn't the sort of chap to let a little matter such as flying under a bridge interfere with good reconnaissance photographs. The bridge rushed closer as I got right down on the deck, the tips of the propellers only a few feet (I hoped) from the water, and then the clear view which I had into the main waterfront of Haugesund was slightly interrupted by three somethings hanging down from the arch of the bridge. They came into focus as three hefty-looking wire ropes dangling down from the stonework, each one of them capable of ripping off a wing. It just wasn't on; I didn't feel like a trip to the knacker's yard yet. As I hauled back with all my might on the control column I yelled, 'It's like the Tay Bridge, Bill. I'm going over the top again.' And fervently hoped that I was. As the nose of the Hudson rose in the climb it obscured the view and I sweated out the next few seconds hoping that the tearing impact would not come and also conscious of a clattering noise in the cockpit area. Then the parapet flashed past a few feet below the port engine. We'd made it.

I eased out of the climb and rammed her into a steep left turn out to sea just in case the gunner was still in business, then climbed sedately away. I became aware of a furious-faced Bill struggling up the stairs from the nose, still with the heavy camera in his hand. I gathered that the clattering noises I'd heard as we swept over the bridge had been Bill and the camera descending the stairs. I must have pulled three or four g to get over that bridge and Bill, caught unaware by the massive increase of force incurred, tumbled or, more accurately, was rammed down the stairs, still with his precious camera in his hand. From being his normal weight as he cranked away at the camera he would suddenly have weighed about 500 lbs two seconds later. It was, of course, too much for any human being to withstand and down he went. From the look on his almost puce face I gathered he'd had what the ballooning world would call a 'hard landing'.

'Can't you, for Christ's sake, fly *under* a bloody bridge for a change,' he bellowed. 'You nearly broke my bloody neck.'

'Sorry Bill.'

'Sorry? Is that all you can bloody well say. You chicken out of every bloody bridge you see and all you can say is "Sorry".' He really was mad.

'Look, Bill, that's four "bloodys" in a row. If I'd taken you under that bridge you really *would* have broken your bloody neck. There were some damn great ropes hanging down from it. They'd have taken the wings off us and then you'd have had a bit more to grumble about.'

Bill looked slightly mollified and we climbed away in silence. I sniffed. 'Can you smell something?' I said.

'Not particularly,' said Bill. He was still in a bit of a huff. 'Oh. . . .You mean, like hot metal?

'Like hot metal, Bill. Get Corporal Purves off the wireless set and Gilbert out of turret and have a good hunt round. Take the hand fire extinguisher with you.'

As Bill and Purves vanished into the cabin I slid back the emergency panel in the floor to expose the engine fire-extinguishers and then did a rapid check of the instrument panel. Everything seemed O.K. with the engines but the smell of burning and hot metal increased and thin smoke started to come in through the cabin heating vents.

Bill came back into the cockpit.

'I can't see anything wrong back there,' he said. 'We've had the inspection panels out of the floor and the bomb-bay looks O.K. It must be from the engines.'

'Nothing showing on the dashboard yet,' I said. 'Go over the checks with me.' I did a complete run-through of the instruments, Bill riding shotgun on me. We were very thorough indeed; we had the incentive. As I checked Bill confirmed each instrument: Oil temperatures and pressures, revolutions, boost, cylinder head temperatures, exhaust gas analysers, fuel pressures, hydraulic and auto pilot pressures, all seemed O.K.

'Well, there's nothing wrong there, anyway,' said Bill.

'Yet,' I said.

I leaned forward as far as I could, twisted my head backwards and looked into the port engine cowling. Everything seemed in order. 'Take a look at the starboard engine, Bill,' I said.

Bill did so. 'This is it!' he cried. 'Come and look!'

I put in the autopilot and joined him at the window. The whole of the crankcase of the starboard engine was a streaming mass of green engine oil. 'Right, Bill. We've got a bullet in that lot somewhere. I'll take her up to 3,000 feet and stick around while we sort it out. If we get on fire we might as well stay over the land until we know whether or not we can control it. If we can't we'll bale out over land. No point in going out to sea, the aircraft will be a total loss anyway and there's no point in getting our feet wet. It's bloody cold down there. Tell Gilbert to get back in the turret and keep a good look-out for Huns.'

The oil continued to pour out, the smell of hot metal increased and the oil temperature rose to a dangerous level. 'I'm shutting down the starboard engine, Bill. If we run it much more it might catch fire. No point in ruining the engine, it'll seize if we go on much longer.'

'O.K., Dopey. She'll fly O.K. on one.'

I opened up the port engine a couple of inches of boost, trimmed on a bit of left rudder and shut down the starboard engine, putting the Hamilton propeller into coarse pitch to reduce the drag. I left the ignition on as I didn't want to oil up the plugs and we might need that engine in an emergency if we were jumped by any Luftwaffe boys who'd had an early breakfast. Within a few minutes the hot metal smell and the smoke had vanished and it looked as though we were in good enough shape to go home.

'Give me a course for home, Bill. You'll have to allow for some extra port drift as we're on one engine.'

Bill came up with the answer and we set off home. The Hudson performed well on one engine, the first aircraft I'd ever flown that did. With the good engine running well below full power it hauled us along at 115 knots. We still had our bombs on board but there was no point in jettisoning them as the machine was coping well. I flew manually as I felt that there might be damage to the autopilot system and, because it was such a strong system, capable of putting all the controls into full deflection if it was fed the wrong information, I felt safer doing the driving myself. I'd had an experience as a navigator when the pilot put in the autopilot without lining up his rudder indices, so George (the universal name in the RAF for the automatic pilot) obliged, put on full rudder and nearly put us into a flick roll, which would have torn the wings off. By the time the pilot got control again we had got well past the vertical and I'd been rolled round the cockpit just like poor old Bill this morning. I didn't want that happening on top of a duff engine.

With a fair amount of left rudder trim, helped by a bit of aileron to keep the left wing down a bit, she flew comfortably and I could relax as the oil and cylinder head temperatures of the starboard engine had now fallen away and the smell of burning had gone. With the starboard propeller windmilling we crabbed our slow way across the North Sea to Leuchars, 350 miles away. About half-way home, a Hudson of C Flight overhauled us but carried on when we assured it, on our signalling lamp, that all was well.

Just for safety we turned on the starboard engine again on final approach and used it for the last hundred yards or so of the landing, and for taxying in to the hangar, as the aircraft would need some engine repairs and the bullet holes in the fuselage would need patching. In fact the damage was slight — a bullet had sliced through an external oil pipe which was easily replaced and the riggers soon patched up the fuselage. The aircraft was serviceable next day, in fact, and we flew her that night on a trip to Frederickshavn, in Denmark.

Chapter 4

'Reconnaissance at *night'* I queried. 'We're not bats.'

'Noun or adverb?' countered the Intelligence Officer in the Ops Room. (He was an Oxbridge type.)

'Er . . . ' (I wasn't hot on grammar, syntax and so forth).

Bill intervened. 'Adverb for Dopey, noun for me. Dopey's as crazy as a coot at times, but I can't see in the dark like the nocturnal, mouse-like quadruped with metacarpals extended to form the framework for membraneous wings that he referred to.'

The I.O., quite justifiably in my opinion, ignored him. 'Full moon,' he stated flatly.

'Eh?'

'I said "Full moon",' he repeated. 'You don't have to be a bat.'

'But what on earth can anyone see at night, even by a full moon, that's of the slightest use to the war effort?'

'How about the *Admiral Scheer* for starters?' said the I.O. (That was a pocket-battleship.)

'Oh, no' said Bill. Or it may have been some other four-letter word.

'We've lost track of the *Scheer,'* said the I.O. 'She's been in the Baltic working up recently and she's vanished from our recce photos so she may well be on her way out. We'd like you to go and look for her and about the only place the photo-recce boys haven't cased throroughly is Frederikshavn in Denmark. The information is wanted urgently and we think there's enough moon to justify a night search.'

I walked over to the chart of the North Sea on the wall and did some measuring. 'It's about 470 nautical miles to Frederikshavn,' I said to the Intelligence Officer (it was my turn to navigate). 'That's a fair trip, about 1,000 miles there and back by the time we've messed about.'

He looked a bit embarrassed. 'Well, actually, it's a little further really. We don't want you to fly over Denmark on the way in to Frederikshavn as we don't want them to have any warning of your approach. We'd like you to slip north-east up the

Skagerrak, well away from land, and then turn south-south west into the Kattegat to come in to Frederikshavn direct from the sea. If they think there are any reconnaissance aircraft about she might slip out to sea at the first warning and we'll have lost her again. *If* she's there, that is. But we'd like to know one way or the other. We realise it's a long trip but you will increase your range by leaving three of your bombs behind. You'll carry one 250 lb semi armour-piercing bomb only, just in case she's there.'

'Well, it's better than nothing, I suppose,' I said. 'Good thing that it will be me who'll be aiming it. If it was Bill he'd probably hit the royal palace at Copenhagen.'

'Quite. Er, complete wireless silence until you've done the recce, then signal us the result immediately. You can come straight home across Jutland when you've finished.'

'You bet.'

We got away from Leuchars before nightfall and I had a good hour of daylight for getting drifts and checking on my navigation so that, after the sun went down, I felt that we were accurately on track. The moon eventually arose in a cloudless sky and the North Sea became a very romantic place indeed. There wasn't much I could do for an hour or so so I sat in isolation in the nose and watched the play of the moon on the waves below, letting my thoughts run on.

Joan, now a fully qualified WAAF MT driver, had been posted to Lossiemouth, up on the Moray Firth. We corresponded occasionally and I saw her on the odd time when she got home on a 48-hour pass. Everything was still very platonic but I enjoyed her company and that of her family; it really took me away from the war. Funnily enough, Bill had been doing a bit of a line for some time past with a cousin of Joan's but that, too, seemed to have fallen through. We were obviously not the world's greatest lovers, Bill and I. The WAAFs had altered camp life a lot, of course. As we were all regular Air Force types who took a bachelor establishment for granted it had been an immense change to have women on the station. When it was announced that we were to have an establishment of WAAFs the reaction was, surprisingly, not entirely in favour. The two squadrons, my own 233, and 224, having been together for three years now had got well used to each other's company. The RAF was far from being celibate, of course, there were numerous complaints to the contrary, and I had been a bit shaken by some of the goings on when I first joined. But, with a war on, it seemed to some of us more seemly, for want of a better word, to conduct the war in male isolation in our bachelor world and to seek our female companionship off the camp. There was a pretty good spirit at Leuchars, which was one of the best stations in the RAF, and the WAAFs would inevitably break up this unity. They did. We all preened ourselves and strutted about to impress the newcomers and the romances flourished. Things had changed greatly but, eventually, even the die-hards such as myself were converted and life settled down to complete normality. If you count a war as normal activity, of course.

The earlier WAAF officers had obviously been chosen for their matronly and gorgonistic qualities. They guarded and fussed over the morals of their airwomen and let it be known, as they strode about the Mess, that they weren't having any nonsense from whipper-snappers (eyeing the pilot fraternity) trying to get *their* girls in the family way. Unfortunately for them the girls themselves appeared to have little aversion to such nonsense and life flowed smoothly on its heterosexual way. Later on, much younger WAAF officers appeared. These were not the administrators of the mass of airwomen but held semi-specialised jobs of their own such as cypher officers, adjutants, equipment officers and so on. They were a new breed and rounded off the cross-section of life so that an RAF station was a pretty well-balanced community. The airwomen's trades multiplied enormously from jobs such as waitresses in the Mess and transport drivers to parachute packers, clerks, equipment assistants, even (greatly daring) batwomen, and later in the war nearly every job there was. They eventually finished up as fitters, riggers and armourers working on the aircraft and did a tremendous job of work. In no other country of all the combatants, Axis powers or Allies, did women make such a contribution as did the women of Britain.

It was the transport drivers who came into close contact with us as they drove us to and from our dispersed aicraft to the hangars and Ops Room. 'Crasher' Renwick, who drove for 233 Squadron, had earned her nickname from an occasion when she took a senior RAF officer into a brick wall, inflicting a fair amount of damage on car and wall but not, fortunately, on the occupants. After her initial prang she became a good driver and we aircrew spent many a quiet period off duty sitting in the front of her 15 cwt Bedford chatting her up. She had, unfortunately, rather bad taste and eventually married an Army officer, of all things, but the RAF, generous to a fault, never really held it against her. After our trips to Norway she had to listen to many, no doubt embellished, accounts of our single-handed combats against the might of the Luftwaffe but it had little softening-up effect, unfortunately.

The intercom came to life with a click. 'You asleep, Dopey?' asked Bill. 'If we carry on this course much longer we're going to be in Sweden.'

'Denmark, actually, Bill. We're still pointing at Denmark but I'll be turning you up into the Skagerrak towards Sweden soon. Just trust Uncle Dopey, he never lets you down.'

'Except over bridges,' muttered Bill. (He'd got quite a sore elbow after our little junket at Haugesund yesterday.)

I ran a swift check on my navigation. 'Not to worry, Bill. You've eight minutes before the next change of course, which will be left on to oh-six-three degrees magnetic. I'll give you a shout.'

I spent the next few minutes checking and rechecking our future changes of course and sorted out our course for home after the job was finished in case there was any hassle. It might save a gallon or two of petrol to be able to leave the scene on an accurate course home. I called Bill.

'O.K. Bill. Alter course 32 degrees port on to oh-six-three magnetic. You'll be on this course for about 20 minutes before we turn east for a while. Then south-south-west for Frederikshavn.'

'Oh-six-three magnetic it is,' confirmed Bill as he swung left.

Forty minutes later we were running towards Frederikshavn at about 500 feet. I switched on the intercom. 'Captain to crew. We'll be at Frederikshavn in about three minutes and with this moon we should be able to see enough to distinguish between any merchant ships and the *Scheer*. She's 12,000 tons, with fairly straight-cut upperworks in two lumps. She's got six four-inch anti-aircraft guns which won't amount to anything tonight, and eight three-pounders and ten machine-guns which might. If anything like the latter shoot at us it's probably the *Scheer*. Keep a good look-out.'

As I came up the stairs I felt the aircraft yaw as the gunner swung his turret forward. Corporal Purves came off the wireless set and stood alongside me at the windows. I clicked on the intercom. 'Frederikshavn coming up now. She's all yours, Bill. Give us a good view.'

'How low do you want?' asked Bill.

'As low as you feel like. We want to make sure of the job, but keep high enough to clear any odd things like church steeples and wireless masts.'

'What about bridges?' enquired Bill innocently. 'Over or under them?' (He'd got bridges on the brain, this chap).

The harbour was sweeping past below us. In the moonlight I couldn't see anything remotely resembling a naval vessel. Bill turned and came in a bit lower for the second run north. An automatic gun opened up on us. Just one gun and a 40 mm by the rate of the muzzle flashes, I reckoned. One nice thing about bright moonlight is that, apart from being great for romances and so on, the tracers and incendiaries don't show up so much; there's a lot of truth in the saying what the eye doesn't see the heart doesn't grieve over. No point in telling Bill about the gun as it looked as though the gunner couldn't hit the floor with his hat without the aid of a searchlight.

'We'll do one more run, Bill, a bit lower if you like.'

Bill did a daisy-clipping effort across the harbour mouth and then went into an immediate, and very steep, climbing turn. An unkind person might have called it more of a clambering swerve than a climbing turn, a bit on the hairy side. I wondered if he was trying to pull a Haugesund on me and send me rattling down the stairs. If so, he'd lost: I was still on my feet.

'Just saving fuel,' grinned Bill. 'Course for home, please.'

'Two-eight-six magnetic, you son of a bitch.'

'Two-eight-six magnetic it is, Dopey.'

I wrote a message and handed it to the wireless operator: '*Scheer* definitely not in Frederikshavn.' In a few minutes confirmation of its receipt came back and I joined Bill in the cockpit as the flat Jutland landscape sailed past underneath us, and checked on my navigation. We flew more or less over Aalborg aerodrome and I considered lobbing our bomb into one of the hangars but we were unfamiliar with Denmark, Norway being our normal beat, and I didn't know just what state of invasion they were in; I might kill some Danes. So we carried on and I got a good fix on the Jutland coast before we set off across the sea for home.

We dropped the bomb when away from the land to ease our load. I watched if fall away but it soon disappeared from sight and I didn't see it hit the sea. We droned silently on through the brilliance of the moonlit night. It was the sort of moon that, four months later, the people of Britain would know as a 'Bomber's moon' as the Heinkels and Dorniers swarmed over the land and set fire to the cities. There was little more that I could do in the navigation line until we got nearer the Scottish coast, when I could get a bearing from Leuchars. The recce at Frederikshavn had interrupted my train of thought and I went back to thinking about the WAAFs. It was painfully obvious that I wasn't having a devastating effect on them, the total number I'd swept off their feet so far having totalled zero. There was Joan, who still held pride of place, and then our driver Crasher. Both 'good friends,' and then, to cap it all, there had been Susan the other day. We'd been diverted to Dyce, Aberdeen, through bad weather and had to stay the night. I was chatting up a far from ugly Assistant Section Officer called Susan and getting on quite well, I thought. The dice were loaded a bit on my side as they still flew Ansons at Dyce while I flew the death-defying Hudsons all the way to Norway and back and I managed to shoot a modest line about it to Susan before leading on to more important things such as forwarding my progress with her.

'The trouble with Welshmen,' said Susan suddenly, ruining my evening 'is that they all have souls.'

I tried my damnedest to look as though I hadn't one, swigging my beer in extrovert style. Maybe she was hinting that she was more interested in bodies in which case I was 100 per cent behind her, though 100 per cent on top of her would have conveyed my feelings more accurately. I didn't manage to get it across. Susan put down her glass. 'Well, thanks for the drink, Dopey,' she said and went over and talked to, of all people, an *Anson* pilot.

I was probably better sticking to my hobby of collecting antique firearms. I had a very fine cased pair of flintlock duelling pistols which I'd bought a year before for half a week's pay, and which I brought out at Mess parties after the senior officers had gone to bed, firing off blank charges which made a considerble boom and produced dense clouds of smoke. I took the precaution of firing off one at a time only, so that I always had one loaded pistol with which to protect myself from being disarmed by the more timorous characters. To some extent they were a squadron asset as they definitely gave us the edge over 224 Squadron. And recently, after haggling, I had acquired an 1856 Beaumont-Adams percussion revolver from an ironmonger in St. Andrews. I finally gave in to his exorbitant price of 30 shillings when he offered to throw in a part-used can of Smokeless Diamond sporting powder. I used only black powder in my duelling pistols but the ironmonger assured me that this smokeless powder would work equally well. Unfortunately I took him on trust, loaded an oversize bullet into the protesting gun, pointed it at wall, pressed the trigger, and immediately wished I hadn't. With a thunderous roar the grossly overloaded gun went off and spun backwards out of my hand, the safety catch taking a goodly lump out of a finger as it went. It landed about 20 yards behind me and was still in one piece, a tribute to the Victorian gunmakers of Birmingham.

The incident put me off smokeless powders in a big way and I decided to get rid of the stuff but it seemed an awful waste just to pour it away. A few days earlier, on one of my walks, I had found a wasps' nest built into the ground. Through the one-inch entrance hole wasps skittered busily to and fro. Wasps are, poor devils, enemies of society, which was a good enough excuse. I took the tin of smokeless plus the flask of black powder from my duelling pistols and set off for the nest. As it was a warm day I took off my tunic before going to work. I poured in the smokeless powder until the nest was full then laid a foot-long trail of black powder as a fuse. This would take a few seconds to burn and would give me time to get to a safe distance. I lit the end of the train with a match and noticed that it seemed to be burning rather quickly, so much so that before I could get off my haunches I saw the ground a foot from my face begin to crack and open up. The pressure wave and the stinging, tearing particles of earth and grit arrived at the same time. I found myself on my back, obviously blinded for life, with my eyes, ears, nose and mouth full of grit and in a fair amount of pain. In time, it subsided to bearable proportions and I found I could open my eyes and that I could still see. To say that I was considerably shaken was to put it mildy. I sat up. A large hole in the ground was all that remained of the wasps' nest; it had entirely vanished. I stood up, collected my tunic and the empty powder tins and prepared to stagger back to the Mess. Then, like a bolt from the blue, I had a coronary attack, which is a truly dreadful thing to have happen to you at the age of 21.

Most of you will be familiar with the symptoms of a coronary — the burning pain over the heart, radiating towards the left arm and so on. But I was quite unprepared for the extensiveness of the area over which the pain spread and the for the incredibly burning aspect of it. I was obviously having a very severe attack. But what on earth were the pains doing round my navel and up near my *right* armpit? Something was up. I opened up the front of my shirt to see a dozen or two half-stunned wasps crawling feebly over my chest, where they had been blown by the force of the explosion. As they recovered they reacted in the only way they knew and drove in their stings. I tore off my shirt and beat the survivors to death.

I became aware of a high-pitched noise in my ears. the

intercom was alive. 'Hey, Dopey, what the hell's up? You *are* down there in the nose?'

'No, Bill, I've fallen overboard. What's cooking?'

'I've called you twice already. Are you asleep or something?'

'No. Just thinking.'

'Well, could you by any chance think of an Estimated Time of Arrival at Leuchars?'.

'I'll try, Bill.'

I called him up a few minutes later. 'ETA Leuchars 0152 hours. Tomorrow morning, that is. I'll ask for a bearing in 20 minutes but I think we're pretty well on track.'

There was no hurry. It was still a beautiful, moonlit night and I wondered if Bill realised what a historic piece of North Sea he was flying over. As I looked down at the sea the moontrack lay as a silvery-golden band on the gently rippling surface, the remainder of the sea a luminant leaden grey. And it was in this patch of sea just about 24 years ago, in our fathers' war, and at about this time of night, that the battleships and battle cruisers of Jellicoe and Beatty were thundering through the night to rendezvous with each other in the prelude to the Battle of Jutland, fought near the Horns Reef not many miles to the south of us. Never since Trafalgar had such British naval might been at sea and never again was such a weight of metal capable of being assembled by our Navy. The first, and only, sea battle between Dreadnought battleships was fought on 31 May 1916 in these waters and despite the tremendous slugging match between the enormous guns, which could wreak such dreadful damage on their targets, the short-term result was inconclusive. It was, as had been Trafalgar, a battle of battle-fleets and the thinking of the commmanders, whatever elements of originality they introduced themselves, was basically that of a formal, set-piece shoot-out.

The mightiest vessels afloat, the battleships and battle cruisers of the post-Dreadnought era were really a pain in the neck for their owners. Like Everest, they were there, and everybody had them so everybody had to keep on having them. It would have been a bold junior officer who queried the wisdom of their existence. Of about 30,000 tons displacement, the battleships carried eight 15-inch guns as a main armament, and a forest of smaller stuff, six-inch and downwards, and they could do about 26 knots. No other type of surface vessel could deal with them. The battle cruiser was developed from an identical ship but could sail up to 30, and even 32, knots, the idea being that it could catch up with cruisers and blow them out of the water. The battle cruiser achieved this speed at the sacrifice of armour protection, it wasn't armoured all that much better than a cruiser. Our latest battleship the *Prince of Wales* was of about 33,000 tons displacement and carried 12,000 tons of armour plating, an enormous weight. The battle cruiser would have only a few thousand tons of much thinner plate and could really only withstand the projectiles fired by ships of up to heavy cruiser type with eight-inch guns. If it was involved in a formal line of battle then a 15-inch shell from an enemy went straight into the hull and, as at Jutland, just one hit could blow up a whole ship if it was in the magazine. Despite the slaughter of the battle cruisers at Jutland the navy still had three of them — the *Hood,* the *Renown* and the *Repulse.* It was to be another year before *Hood* was blown up by *Bismark*, a predictable result once the lightly-armoured ship had met that leviathan.

The Achilles heel of all these ships was, of course, the submarine and its torpedo; to these they were vulnerable, so the immensely valuable vessels could not move without an escort of cruisers and destroyers to scout ahead and clear the way for them, and this tied down an awful lot of ships. They were naval white elephants. Latterly, of course, the aeroplane had arrived to further bedevil the existence of naval ships. Nobody yet knew just how effective they would be. True, they could carry torpedoes but they were, as yet, only 18-inch torpedoes as against the standard naval 21-inch which packed a much greater punch. Bombs were equally an unknown factor. Launched in a low level attack they had only the speed of the aircraft, perhaps a couple of hundred feet per second, so that they could not penetrate armour plate. Launched from a great height so that they could attain an adequate speed for penetration, the methods of aiming were such that it was extremely difficult to hit even a stationary ship. To hit a moving ship in a high level attack was almost an impossibility.

But the aircraft would soon make its point. At Taranto, in November 1940, the Swordfish and Albacore aircraft of the Fleet Air Arm would severely damage, or sink, several Italian battleships and, in May 1941, the mighty *Bismark* would be slowed adequately by an aircraft torpedo for her to be caught by surface ships and disposed of. The final, conclusive, proof was the sinking of the *Prince of Wales* and the *Repulse* by the Japanese. After that, naval thinking just had to acknowledge that the aircraft had arrived and that the large capital ship was a real problem child and had to be replaced by the aircraft carrier as the capital ship of the future.

In 1940 the conventional battleships being built for the German navy, the *Bismark* and the *Tirpitz,* were not completed and their heavy units consisted of the ingenious 26,000-ton ships the *Scharnhorst* and the *Gneisenau,* and the 12,000-ton armoured ships (pocket-battlships as they were called) the *Deutschland, the Admiral Scheer* (whom we'd been looking for tonight) and the *Graf von Spee* (sunk at the Battle of the River Plate). Both classes of ship carried the 11-inch gun as their main armament. The *Scharnhorst* and the *Gneisenau* could do 30 knots and the pocket-battleships 26 knots.

In the permutations which could arise in sea warfare both these classes of ship were at a decided advantage. A 15-inch gun battleship could not catch the *Scharnhorst* or the *Gneisenau* as both those ships could run away as fast as they felt like. A cruiser, which had approximately the same speed as them, would get blown out of the water by their heavier guns if it attempted to close the range and could also be attacked by them as often as not. The pocket-battleships could be caught by our faster cruisers but, again, they had the vastly superior 11-inch gun with which to ward off any eight-inch or six-inch gunfire. This war was not going to produce any battlefleet action between the British and German navies; it was going to be a matter of commerce-raiding by the Germans and the formation of numbers of hunter-killer groups on our part to hunt them down. We had our first success at the Battle of the River Plate when the *Graf von Spee* was damaged enough by our eight-inch and six-inch cruisers the *Exeter,* the *Ajax* and the *Achilles* to force her to run into Montevideo, and, eventually to scuttle herself. When you consider that the weight of broadside fired by the *Spee* exceeded the *combined* broadsides of all three British ships in the ratio of about two to one, with the over riding range and power of the 11-inch guns as the dominant factor, you can realise the problem they set us and also, of course, the courage of the men who had run the gauntlet of heavy-gun fire before they could get within fighting range. I didn't fancy that kind of warfare at all; the air suited my tastes better.

Still, moonlight or no moonlight, romantic or otherwise, the WAAFs and wasps would have to wait. I went up the stairs to the wireless operator, passing Bill in the lambent semi-darkness of his cockpit, the instrument bank in front of him a mass of luminous dials, the only sign of movement a slow oscillation of the synchroscope as one or other of the engines in turn gained or lost a few revolutions. As I stepped over the main spar to the wireless cabin I couldn't help but think that Petrus van Schendel, who'd been dead these seventy years or more, might well have painted the scene that I looked at, with Corporal Purves's face softly illuminated by the dim, orange-red light of his operating lamp.

'Get me a bearing from Leuchars, would you, Corporal.'

On 24 April the standby Battle Flight of three aircraft was sent off to provide air cover for three of our destroyers somewhere off Bergen. The job was a routine one of keeping away shadowing aircraft and bombers and of putting down any U-boats ahead of their track. The leader and No.3 were from C Flight with Bill and me from B Flight as No. 2. We got away from Leuchars at 0635 hours and must have been very close to the destroyers we were to escort when we were jumped by two Messerschmitt 109s. Our leader turned westwards and dived for the surface of the sea to prevent the 109s from getting underneath us. He went pretty well flat out and Derry Matson at No.3 and I had trouble keeping up with him and in keeping the tight formation desirable for good supporting gunfire from our turrets. We flew the then standard V formation employed in defensive tactics (though a more efficient system would probably have been to fly in line abreast, but we hadn't thought that one up yet) and found that with the leader going so fast we wing men had little power reserve for manoeuvring and our formation got a bit ragged and open. The two disadvantages of this were that the leader's turret guns could give only negligible supporting fire and, of course, that we two wing men received the exclusive output of the 109s' guns.

The golden rule when under attack is to turn towards your attacker, not away from him. The more you turn in towards him the bigger the deflection he has to employ, the more difficult the shot becomes and you also shorten considerably the time during which he can fire effectively. If you turn away from him you can end up presenting him with nil-deflection shot from dead astern, the easiest shot in the book. With two 109s attacking us the leader had a bit of a problem as they stuck out one on each beam and made concerted beam and quarter attacks together, so that, theoretically at least, one would have been as safe flying straight and level all the time on a swings-and-roundabouts principle, but it's difficult thing to persuade yourself to do and we twisted and turned a fair amount. Gunfire damage apart I was much more concerned at the hammering our engines were getting. With six engines running at take-off boost I felt that, sooner or later, at least one engine would pack in and that that aircraft would then have dropped back to be finished off in very short order by the 109s. The slight loss in speed which we would have incurred through coming back a couple of inches in boost pressure would have made little difference as the 109s were 100 mph faster than we were anyway and it would greatly have relieved the strain on the engines, which is a thing that's always at the back of your mind when you've anything up to 400 miles of cold sea to cross in order to get home. However, we were stuck with the situation as it was and we flitted along quite close to the surface (but not too close as it then becomes easy for the attacker to correct his aim from the bullet splashes in the sea) with our gunners getting rid of their ammunition at a rate of knots. Although I preferred it when I was firing my front guns, it was a comfort to hear the turret Brownings rattling away.

After about 25 minutes of potting at us the 109s had obviously finished their ammunition and they sheared off, leaving all three of us flying and apparently in good order (though two of Derry Matson's crew had been wounded.) We took stock and found that all three aircraft *were* in good order despite the half-hour hammering the engines had received, but we had used so much fuel in the action that we had to abandon any idea of providing air cover for the destroyers and hadn't even enough to get home with any degree of safety so we made for Lossiemouth to refuel. A few minutes later we came up with three French destroyers but, again we couldn't help them at all and carried on to Lossiemouth.

Lossie was a grass aerodrome and we landed in a wide V about 100 yards apart. I was on the right and, after we touched down, I took a look at Derry Matson on the left and was dismayed to see that he had developed a noticeable swing to starboard and that it looked as though we were going to collide. I abandoned my grip on the wheel, pulled hard on the brake lever with both hands and trod on full right rudder but, for a long time, it didn't seem to have any effect on Derry's apparently firm intention of ramming us. With the undercarriage shuddering and groaning the Hudson skeetered harshly over the ground until at last we seemed to be slowing down faster than Derry, and, as he slid across me about 20 yards in front of my nose, I noted that his rudders were at full left deflection as, indeed, they should have been in an effort to correct his ham-handed landing. 'It's a fine thing, Bill,' I said when we'd all stopped, 'to arrive home intact after a dusting from a couple of 109s and then nearly get clobbered on the deck by a pal doing a lousy landing!'

'Yes,' said Bill, loosening his grip on the bulkhead, 'typical C Flight effort, the whole bloody trip. Now let's get some fuel and get off home. If we do it quickly we'll be home for lunch.'

I looked out of the window before taxying in and it seemed strange that the hangars, towards which we'd been landing, were nowhere to be seen. I also became aware of the fact that we were left wing low and a glance out of the side window revealed a flat port tyre. Feeling extremely guilty that it was I who had swung into Derry and not him into me (I had swung a good 90 degrees) I switched off the engines and noticed that Derry was still in position about 20 yards away and that he was *right* wing low. *He* had a burst *right* tyre and we'd both been doing an inward swing. We piled out on to the grass and Derry and I apologised for all the harsh things we'd thought about each other. Apart from Derry's two wounded crewmen our two aircraft were little damaged by gunfire but it's amazing how close those 109s had come to writing off two Hudsons and, perhaps their crews, with a couple of bullets in the tyres. If we'd landed in close formation nothing on earth could have stopped Derry and me from slamming into each other at about 100 mph. I had also learned from the incident that the undercart would stand up to some pretty brutal treatment, which was a great comfort in view of those wet wing tanks so near to the engines. And as for the engines themselves they had been magnificent. I was beginning to have great confidence in the Hudson.

The fire engine and ambulance had streaked out to our two stranded aircraft and we hitched a lift back on the fire engine and held a conference on the tarmac. The leader was undamaged so he refuelled and took off immediately for Leuchars to organise a couple of spare wheels for us. As it was obvious that we'd not get away that day we fixed up accommodation in the Mess and I made straight for the MT section and strode in as though I belonged to the place.

'Good morning, Flight Sergeant, is ACW Lawson about?'

'I think so, sir. She should be at one of the 15 cwt Bedfords over there. Er, is anything wrong, sir?'

'No, Chiefy, just wanted a word with her.'

Joan was evidently having a domestic morning. With her sleeves rolled up and a handful of rags in her hand she was cleaning the engine of her 15 cwt. With grubby fingernails, straggling hair and an oil-streaked face she didn't exactly look like the boudoir queen of the old days in St. Andrews. She looked, in fact, far better. It was good to see her smiling face again.

'Hello, Dopey, what on earth are you doing in this part of the world?'

'Oh, just dropped in *en passant,* you know.'

On the pretext of having to organise the repair of my aircraft the co-operative Flight Sergeant lent me Joan and her 15 cwt. After checking with the Duty Pilot that it was O.K. to cross the airfield I took her off on a line-shooting expedition of the battle-scarred Hudsons. With becoming modesty I underplayed the heroic part I had played in the morning's action. I pointed out the bullet holes and the shredded tyre, gave a convincing account of the difficulties of the landing and, on the strength of her oohing and aahing, dated her up for the night in Elgin, that metropolis of the north with its torrid night life.

In the afternoon a Hudson diverted from its patrol and dropped off a couple of spare wheels before setting off for Norway. We got the repairs started and I caught the bus into Elgin. In those early days open association between officers and other-rank WAAFs was still frowned upon and you didn't take WAAFs into the public bar. One made for the 'Residents' Lounge' kind of establishment, which wasn't half the fun; at least the one I picked wasn't. Its utter drabness, dreariness and respectability put the kiss of death into whatever romance I hoped I could inject into my hopeless attempt to switch Joan on. We gave up after a couple of hours. I took her home to her billet and set off to walk the five miles back to Lossiemouth. Having landed with just what I stood up in I had no greatcoat and was soon chilled to the marrow by the cold wind blowing off the Moray Firth, but half-way home a battered jalopy driven by another RAF type picked me up. It seemed that he, too, had had a similar orgy to mine in Elgin. We chewed the cud over the hell of war and just how damned difficult women could be and he dropped me off at the drab wooden hut with its sparsely furnished room where I crept into my cold bed for the night.

I met Bill and Derry at breakfast and, by mid-morning, our aircraft had their new wheels on and we were on our way home. This was about the third occasion on which I'd been diverted to other aerodromes for the night and I decided to assemble an overnight kit when I got back. In St. Andrews I found a tiny compressed-cardboard attaché case about twelve inches by eight and packed it with a spare razor, shaving soap and brush, toothbrush, face flannel, etc., and a spare collar, handkerchief, socks and underpants, bar of chocolate and a Penguin book for passing the time in the more dreary locations. Armed with this I felt ready for anything; though I did look rather like a caricature of a city gent as I boarded my aircraft with this cheap, rather vile-looking, and idiotically small case in my hand. Fortunately this was before the days of the 'image' so I didn't have to worry too much about public opinion and it was put to good use within two days of being assembled. A couple of days later, with Sgt Axe as second pilot, we were doing a search in particularly nasty weather, with ten-tenths cloud at about 250 feet and drizzle reducing the visibility to a miserably unsafe degree when we were radioed to divert to Lossiemouth again before the clag shut right down. We scraped in low over the coast at Lossie and parked thankfully on the deck, to find that Joan had a 48-hour leave pass and was home in St. Andrews!

It was to be some days before we got home again. The next day the bad weather continued to make flying impossible but an urgent telephone call from Leuchars told me to get up to Wick as soon as it was safe to fly and to put myself at the disposal of 269 Squadron, whose station it was. It started to clear during the night and we got off from Lossie at 0630 hours on May Day, landing 25 minutes later at Wick to find the aerodrome packed with Hudsons and Beauforts and the Ops Room a seething mass of aircrew, many of them from 233 and 224. There was a flap on as the Army was having a really bad time in Northern Norway, were obviously being pushed into the sea, and the Navy was stretched to hell trying to keep them supplied. The Hun had, by now, every airfield in Norway. The 18 Gladiators of 263 Squadron which had flown off from the aircraft carrier *Glorious* on 24 April to operate under appalling conditions from the frozen surface of Lake Lesjaskog had, by the 28th, all been destroyed by bombing but, not before they had shot down 14 of the Luftwaffe. There were no more British aircraft in Norway. (Though there would be within three weeks, when we got some Gladiators and Hurricanes into Bardufoss, where they fought magnificently during the withdrawal to Narvik. With no previous experience of deck-landing and with no arrester hooks on their aircraft the pilots eventually landed them on to the aircraft carrier *Glorious* on the final evacuation. Tragically, the *Glorious* was sunk on 8 June, when on her way home, and the two squadrons perished almost to a man).

But, on May Day, the nearest RAF was our hastily assembled mob at Wick. I had landed at 0700 hours and left Sgt Axe to get the tanks topped up while I went to the Operations Room. I had just about got in when I was nabbed by my Flight Commander to complete a Battle Flight of three and, by 0810 hours we were in the air and on our way to Trondheim to provide air cover to the mass of naval and transport vessels in the area. The details of the trip have faded in my memory but we were stretching our range a bit to help out the poor devils in that area as we flew for 7 hours, 20 minutes, which did not leave much reserve for bad weather or high-speed combat manoeuvres should we become involved. The next morning we went across and flew anti-sub and anti-bomber escort around a couple of our cruisers and their attendant destroyers, again returning to Wick so that we could get up to these high latitudes.

That second night at Wick was my first, and only, experience of seeing the Aurora Borealis — the Northern Lights. I had left the Mess to go to my quarters when I became aware of darting coloured lights in the sky to the north. From the low horizon sheets and waves of multi-coloured lights flickered and flowed across the heavens. In the dead silence of that cold northern night it was quite eerie, watching that mute and lovely display. I walked further out on to the aerodrome to ensure that my silent world would not be disturbed and then, quite suddenly, it was gone and I went back to my quarters quietly and wonderingly.

The third day was to be our last at Wick. Three of us took off to do a sweep into the Skagerrak to look for, and bomb, a German convoy reported in the area, after which we were to return home. We did not find it and abandoned the search when, too near the coast and its Messerschmitts for comfort, the cloud cover lifted and the visibility became unlimited. By now the persistent attrition of our numbers, and the fact that we were quite obviously on a losing wicket, had resulted in a more cautious attitude in balancing risk against probable benefit. Our normal attack against a soft-skinned ship was a low level run-in at about 100 feet. While this greatly increased the chance of a hit it was the most dangerous attack from the aircraft's point of view as it was the light flak (light in calibre, that is — the machine guns and 20 and 40 mm cannon — which were usually mounted in great numbers on ships) that knocked us out of the sky. Out of the tens of thousands of rounds shot at you in a low level shipping attack quite a few went home. The heavy anti-aircraft guns rarely connected (if they *did* the result was a foregone conclusion) as the problems for the gunners were considerable. Nevertheless they did have an effect on one's morale, the belching black smoke and red flame from the muzzle not being conducive to peace of mind. Apart from the sheer volume of the light flak, a high proportion

Junker 88, the aircraft which we allowed to get on our tail at Stavanger on 17 April 1940, as we thought it was a Blenheim. (I.W.M.)

Bristol Blenheim. Note similarity to the Ju88.

19 April 1940. The bridge at Haugesund that I tried to fly under in an attempt to get away from a too-good German ground machine-gunner. Gives a clear view of the bridge. (Normanns Kunstforlag A/S)

This gives a more accurate idea of what we had to contend with as there were some ships obstructing the entrance, though not this many. (Haugesunds Avis)

A Messerschmitt 109 shooting at me on 24 April 1940. Photograph taken from the leader of the formation. Unknown to me at the time, he burst one of my tyres.

'Gunfire Flat'. Burst tyres normally caused the aircraft to swing in the direction of the flat tyre after landing. The noise of a tyre bursting as a result of a gunshot is not normally heard above the engine noise so that by the time the pilot is aware of the swing, it is already well established and can be difficult to deal with at times, especially if the aircraft has suffered other battle damage. It throws a great strain on the undercarriage leg. Note large exhaust pipe of the 1,100 horse power engine.

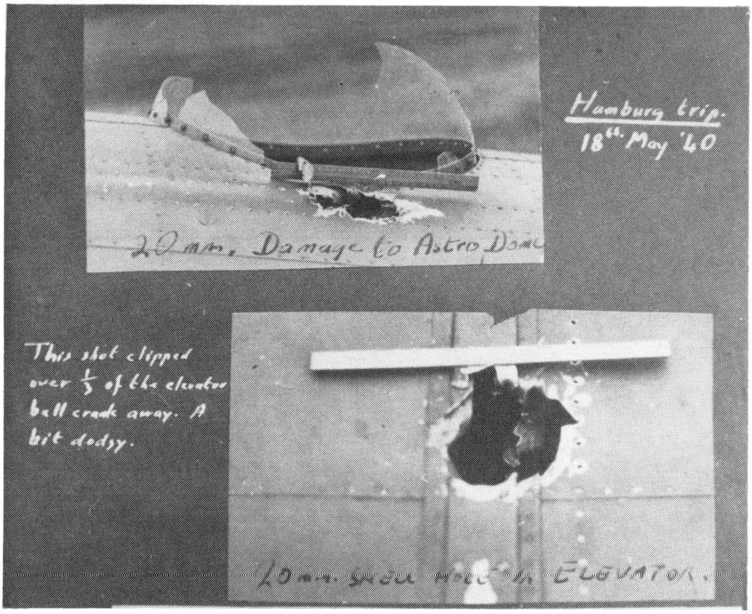

18 April 1940. Some of the 20 mil damage incurred during the low level raid on Hamburg. The shot that caused most concern was that in the elevator, which weakened the elevator control by 33 per cent.

Damage to wing, probably from 40 mm explosive shell. This was done, I think, by a British cruiser to the Hudson of Pilot Officers O'Neill and Rothwell of 224 Squadron who were carrying out protective escort to the ship. 'Fire first, and ask questions afterwards' was the motto of quite a few Navy gunners. They certainly fired at me on at least two occasions. (I.W.M.)

was of tracer and incendiary, so that one saw the smoke trails reaching out at you like lethal fingers wanting to tear the guts out of you. As long as one saw an elongated trail coming up it wasn't so bad; it was probably going to miss. But when it foreshortened, to become a wavering blob of smoke, they you knew that it probably had your name on it and was coming too fast for any avoiding action to be of use. And hits from 20 mm and 40 mm shells could inflict lethal damage on an aircraft. Even minor damage could be a great embarrassment as we had quite a few hundred miles to come home after an attack.

Fighter cover, the 'umbrella', much modified our tactics. Then it was virtual suicide to do a low attack and cloud cover was essential for survival, the height of the cloud dictating the height of the attack. One just had to be able to nip into the safety of the cloud as soon as possible. If the fighter pilot was a good shot (and they all weren't, thank heaven) they you were a sitting duck in clear skies, with him able to dictate the entire action through his superior speed and possessing about twenty times the fire power. We had the greatest respect for the Messerschmitts though I did once, for a short time only, ignore their menace. We were stooging northwards along the Norwegian coast when Bill came bounding up the stairs from the nose and, waving an arm dramatically to starboard, yelled, '109s. Six of them.'

I looked, and saw nothing. 'You're seeing things, old boy. Now do be a good chap and get on with the navigation.'

Bill went back to his hovel in the nose but was back in ten seconds. 'Morning, Bill. Haven't seen you for some time. Keeping well?'

'For Christ's sake,' he bellowed, 'Messerschmitts. Six of the bastards. ONE OH BLOODY NINES. LOOK!'

I looked, and saw nothing except the magnificent Norwegian coastline that I was coming to know so well. 'Liver spots, old horse.'

Bill got really agitated at this so I decided I'd have to humour him and called up the gunner, 'Gilbert,' I said, 'Mr Tacon says he can see six 109s about green oh-five-oh. Have a look, will you?'

I felt the Hudson yaw as the turret swung round. A few seconds later Gilbert came up on the intercom. 'Six 109s it is sir, green oh-five-oh, 1,000 feet up, closing.'

I couldn't see a damned thing. 'Give me the glasses, Bill, would you?' I focussed the binoculars and there, sure enough, on our starboard bow about four miles away six 109s were streaming black smoke from their exhausts as they closed the range rapidly.

I spun round, turned on the taps and made cloud cover before they caught up with us.

'Sorry chaps,' I apologised to the crew on the intercom when we were safely tucked up in the cloud, 'Won't occur again.'

I wasn't flying the next day and had a long ponder on the matter. It was a bit of a devil to be going short-sighted at the age of 21 and I'd have to do something about it. In the afternoon I hopped on a bus into St. Andrews, found a civilian optician and, within two hours, had been fixed up with a compact pair of steel-rimmed spectacles that would cope with any 109 in the book. 'I've over-corrected you a little to allow for further deterioration,' said the optician. At that rate I'd see them before they took off. (I suppose Bill must have sighted those 109s first at about five miles range — the sort of thing you can do in clear atmosphere with good eyesight.)

Well pleased with my day's shopping I returned to Leuchars. I was navigating the next trip and, when we were safely airborne and away from observation, I put on my specs and came up out of the nose to test Bill's reaction.

'What the hell are those things?' said Bill, taking his helmet off for easier conversation.

'What do they look like, mate?' I said. 'They're Mark 1 glasses. Anti-109 and all that sort of guff.'

'Well, after last time's effort you certainly need them. Must say you look a bit odd in them, though. Whoever heard of a pilot wearing glasses?'

'Well, you've got one now chum and, if you breathe a word to anyone, I'll get myself a new second pilot. A *good* one.'

'O.K. Mum's the word. Are those steel rims the best you could do, though? I'd have lent you a quid for a better pair if I'd known you were so short.'

'Policy, old boy. They're the smallest pair I could get. I can carry these in my top pocket and nobody's any the wiser.'

I tried them out next on Corporal Davies, the wireless operator. On the pretex of discussing bearings with him I sat on the spar and chatted him up for a couple of minutes. Tubby Davies rarely showed visible emotion, taking all things well in his stride. I remembered the time we had the fight with the Heinkel 115. As I fired each burst with my front Brownings he stood up from his seat at the wireless set to see where the tracer was going and sat down immediately the guns stopped firing. A stoical fellow, Tubby. I went back to the nose and Tubby miscalculated in thinking I hadn't put on my helmet with its intercom set. He rang up the gunner.

'Gilly, Edwards is wearing glasses!' 'Jesus! Mind you, he needs them. You were on the last trip, weren't you? If it hadn't been for the rest of us we'd be starting our third day at the bottom of the North Sea. He'll be bringing his crutches next.'

'Bedsocks, too, I shouldn't wonder,' said Tubby. 'It's a bit of a bugger, though, isn't it?'

I clicked on my intercom. 'Captain to crew. I heard that lot. I'm sorry my infirmities cause you such concern but I'm prepared to overlook the matter. There's no point in mentioning it to anyone else, though, is there? Unless you want to fly under the Tay Bridge, or something.' They agreed.

I kept the glasses in my hideous little attaché case as part of my standard flying kit and it was well over a year before the medicos caught up with me when, through circumstances within my control, I ended up with the cap of a 20mm cannon shell in my eye socket and I failed the vision test on my discharge from hospital.

Chapter 5

The war in Europe, known as the 'Phoney War' or 'Sitzkrieg', as no fighting had yet taken place, suddenly exploded into action as Germany invaded France and the Low Countries, and what was to become known as the Battle of France began, leading to our being thrown off the mainland at Dunkirk. We got the news early and the station buzzed with excitement but we hadn't time to get all the information as Lord Louis Mountbatten's destroyer, the flotilla leader *Kelly,* had been torpedoed by an E-boat off Jutland. She was in a bad way but was still afloat and great efforts were being made to get her home. A battle flight of two Hudsons led by Cooper, my Flight Commander, had got airborne well before first light and had shot at two shadowing Dornier 18K flying boats and, throughout the day, we kept three aircraft continuously on air cover round her.

At 1625 hours Sqn Ldr Feeney, our second-in-command, led three of us on the final flight of the day. We arrived to find the *Kelly* with a pronounced list to starboard, the guard rail being under water and half the crew lining the port rail to keep as much weight as possible on that side. She was under tow, and moving very slowly and awkwardly and she seemed to me to be a sitting duck for the Luftwaffe not all that far away to the east. What surprised me as much as anything was the number of ships the Navy were risking in order to salvage her. We had arrived at 1815 hours to find the towing destroyer together with two cruisers and four more destroyers; it seemed an awful lot of ships to put at risk. As soon as we arrived Sqn Ldr Feeney disappeared to the eastward to search an area 20 miles wide by 50 miles deep behind the force for any shadowing aircraft or ships and we did not see him again as, by the time he had completed this task, night had fallen and he could not make contact again. Williams of A Flight and I stayed with the force until nightfall and left them steaming westwards at about 2-3 knots. We landed after a seven-hour trip, and the *Kelly* eventually made it back to the Tyne and was repaired to continue in the dashing kind of service that one associated with Lord Louis, until she was sunk by the Luftwaffe off Crete in 1941.

The start of the Battle of France certainly put the kybosh on any reinforcement of the Norwegian campaign and, from now on, we were on a losing wicket, the evacuation of Norway becoming a foregone conclusion. The Battle of France was to end similarly and even more rapidly, of course. In three weeks the remains of the British army were encircled at Dunkirk and were only extricated with the most amazing good luck to support the courage shown by everyone there. Norway and Dunkirk were the first of the apparently endless series of defeats inflicted on the undermanned and under-equipped British fighting services in the early years of the war. Every man in the services accepted fairly philosophically that he would automatically be fighting against far superior forces and there was nothing he could do to alter it. I'll never forget, when I was home on leave some time in 1940, my eldest brother, a gunner in a Territorial Army unit, proudly showing me his guns, two-pounder anti-tank guns. *Two* pounders, for God's sake! They'd bounce off 90 per cent of the armour of the German Panzer divisions, but I hadn't the heart to disillusion him.

The public were equally used to it, of course, and we weren't spat on in the streets for losing almost every battle we fought. I can only remember one occasion when criticism seemed a bit harsh and that was when I found myself the only RAF type in a railway carriage full of Army who'd obviously, from their conversation, been booted out of France via Dunkirk. From the tone of the talk it was obvious that they had seen their first action and that it had been of short duration. Inevitably the matter of air support came up. Very few of our aircraft were seen by the beleaguered soldiers pinned down on the beaches and I was drawn into the conversation, at first politely, and then with increasing criticism as the soldiers wanted to know where the hell the RAF was at Dunkirk. It was almost in vain that I pointed out that whatever aircraft we could spare would have been five or ten miles inland, where they could infict most damage on the Hun, and that the German aircraft which appeared over the beaches were those which had already (alas too easily in view of their overwhelming numerical superiority) run the gauntlet of the lonely Hurricane fighters to the east. Harking back to our cock-up over the *Suffolk's* bombardment of Stavanger aerodrome, Dunkirk was of course an immeasurably bigger blunder on Hitler's part. By withholding the full weight of his available resources in the vain expectation that we would pack in the war he allowed the majority of the British Army to get out of Dunkirk to fight again.

As the Norwegian war hotted up we were being attacked more and more by German fighters — the Messerschmitt 109 (their equivalent of the Spitfire) and the twin-engined Messerschmitt 110, which was slower but of far greater range, and which could hunt us out more or less wherever we went. As a counter-measure we increased our defensive armament by fitting a mounting for a Lewis gun outside a cabin window on each side. If an attack was imminent one unshipped the Lewis from its stowage and stuck it out of the window on the appropriate side. If the attacker changed sides you could, of course, whip the gun over to the other mounting and carry on firing. This gave the wireless operator or the navigator something to do and kept them happier when under fire. I would have far preferred the simpler and more reliable Vickers K gun in place of the Lewis, but beggars can't be choosers and the Lewis was a useful adjunct. On a reconnaissance off Bergen, Messerschmitts were sighted and I'd hurtled into action on the side Lewis. I gave a trial burst to make sure the gun was working properly but whatever it was that put the wind up us didn't materialise so I hauled the gun inboard. Just then we hit bumpy weather, the gun shot out of its mounting and the muzzle clumped to the floor as I tried to regain my balance. Inevitably I pressed the trigger. In the confines of the cabin the muzzle blast and explosion caused consternation all round, and a hole blown in the floor showed I'd been lucky not to lose a foot. The bullet had gone into the bomb-bay so we felt it advisable to do a thorough check on things. A tracer or incendiary lodged against something solid like a bomb and fizzing away could start something unpleasant. We whipped out the floor inspection panels, opened the bomb doors and had a good squint round. One of the bombs under the blasted floorboard had a score mark on it as though a bullet had bounced off it and, as the bomb doors closed, I spotted the exit hole so all was well. The bullet was by this time safely at the bottom of the sea. Somewhat easier in mind I stowed the Lewis gun and trotted back to the nose to take up my interrupted navigation duties, having to run the gauntlet of a far-from-impressed Bill in the pilot's seat.

'Any more funny tricks up your sleeve?' he asked. 'If so, can you give me a bit more warning next time. You darned nearly burst my ear drums.'

'Scared you a bit, too, I'll bet?' I said cruelly.

'That, too.' said Bill.

A few days later a whole mob of eight complete crews jostled in the Ops Room. 'Get off to North Coates Fitties as soon as you can and report to the Ops Room there,' said our Controller.

'North Coates?' someone queried. 'That's a Bomber Command station. What do they want with us there?'

'You'll no doubt find out as soon as you get there,' said the Controller brightly. 'Your bomb loads have been changed to four two-fifty GPs. Now, off you go. They want you there by 1400 hours for briefing.'

We took off independently and coast-crawled down to North Coates, to be informed at the briefing that we were part of a night-bombing raid. Obviously Bomber Command were as stretched as we were and we were to boost the numbers. This was my first experience of a bomber briefing and I can't say that I was all that pleased with our change of role. In Coastal Command we usually operated alone or in small numbers, in daylight and against a variety of targets about which the information was usually scanty or very hastily assembled, as the war at sea could change very rapidly. It was very much an individual's kind of war. This bomber briefing followed a formalised, set plan, the main purpose of which seemed to be to frighten the life out of you. Guns here, balloons there, recognition signals, flares, flak, radio frequencies this, that and the other and heaven-knows-what-else. One nice thing, however, was Air-Sea Rescue, of which I thoroughly approved. They were in advance of what we had at the other end of the North Sea. The target was oil tanks in Hamburg's dockland and the recommended bombing height was 12,000 feet, which was about 11,800 feet higher than we were used to.

Bill and I lay out in the sun alongside our Hudson (painted on its underside in the attractive Coastal Command silver/white — hardly the thing for night work) and chewed over the information we had. We were very conscientious in those days and it worried me that there wasn't a hope of hitting those tanks from 12,000 feet. In the back of my mind was the idea that, as there would be no barrage balloon cables in the middle of a river (which was an incorrect assumption as it turned out; they had them moored to barges), we could go up the river Elbe at about 500 feet, where they wouldn't be expecting to find an aircraft at night, drop down on to the target and clobber it in a low level attack, then back to the river and away. The trouble was that I had to lead Bill from 12,000 feet down to 500. Easy stages would be the answer, I felt.

Get him down to 8,000 feet for a start, then point out that our maximum speed of 246 mph was achieved at 6,500 feet. Toss in the statement that the Mark IX bomb-sight wasn't all that good at that sort of altitude (an unwarranted slur on the instrument, but Bill probably wouldn't notice), something a little lower, perhaps. And so on. It was going to be a ticklish matter to introduce such an unorthodox method of attack as it's not everyone's idea of a good way to fly an aircraft at night. I racked my brains for some easy way to get the ball rolling when Bill's voice broke in on my reverie.

'You know, Dopey, we'll never hit those tanks from 12,000 feet.'

'Great!' I thought. 'He's at 8,000 feet already, job's one-third done.'

'Like what sort of height do you visualise, man?' I said and kept my fingers crossed. Maybe Bill would remember that 6,500 was our best height. Poor old Bill. It was a shame really. He didn't know what was going to hit him eventually.

'Well,' said Bill in measured tones, 'if you want to *hit* those tanks I'd suggest 300 feet.'

'THREE hundred feet! At bloody night!' I howled. 'You're nuts.'

'Look,' said Bill patiently, 'if we don't get those tanks tonight they'll probably keep us here for days until we've done it. Let's get the job over with and get back home to a civilised war.'

Well, I'd certainly got him down from twelve grand but 300 feet really was the giddy limit. 'Look, Bill,' I said, 'I'm not taking this thing up the river at 300 feet at night. Make it 500 and you've got a deal.'

Bill agreed, but I felt a bit uneasy about the way he'd independently thought out such a heretical idea and made a mental note that I'd have to keep a careful eye on him in future; one damn fool in an aircraft was quite enough, two might be a bit of a luxury.

We didn't mention our scheme to anyone and, at 2125 hours, we got away from the flarepath at North Coates, climbed away like everybody else but stopped at 2,000 feet for the sea crossing. As we approached the Elbe estuary the flak started up on the boys at the normal bombing height but this was of only academic interest to us and we dropped down to 500 feet on autopilot. We had quite a few laughs as we watched the mounting searchlight activity and shell bursts up top and carried on our peaceful way up the river.

'You know, Bill,' I said, not without an element of smugness, 'it's brains and intelligence that's going to win this war. Just look at those poor buggers up there!' Bill and I gazed through the roof panels at a Whitley caught in a searchlight, with shell bursts all round it. 'If he was down here with us he'd be as right as rain.'

'Yes,' said Bill. 'It's a matter of education really.'

As he spoke night vanished in a blinding haze of white light. From Cuxhaven on the south bank a searchlight had got us well and truly fixed. I was completely blinded so I stuck my head below window level then whipped out the autopilot and flew on instruments. More searchlights got on to us and then the light flak started up. As we twisted and turned up the narrowing river the light flak increased in density; we were the only target they had, and the night became aglow with streaks of flame of all colours coming from both banks.

'Brunsbuttel coming up on the north bank!' Bill yelled.

Brunsbuttel is where the Kiel canal runs into the Elbe and there were usually German naval units there, together with their associated defences; a good place to avoid so I made more for the south bank, but it made little difference. Bill said later he counted eleven searchlights on us at one time off Brunsbuttel and the hammering of the light flak multiplied depressingly. As we fled from that concentration of light although we lost a few searchlights, the Hun didn't seem to be running short of guns. As we left one group of guns for another the first series of four or five coloured balls would rise lazily from the ground and float towards us, suddenly increasing in speed and becoming streaks of light a yard long accelerating with amazing suddenness across, above, below and behind us and, occasionally through us with a splintery crash. The hosepiping of the tracer looked so menacing that I ordered Dutch Holland out of the turret. I felt that if he started shooting back they would just shoot straight up his traces and really clobber us. So poor old Dutch had to join Bill and the wireless operator in a nail-biting session as we jinked liked we'd never jinked before — a steep climbing turn to about 500 feet followed by an equally steep diving turn. Allowing for the lag in the altimeter I started to pull out of the dive when it registered 200 feet unless a screech from Bill indicated an earlier pull-out if we weren't to hit the water. At intervals, and with increasing regularity, shots continued to crash through the fuselage and one considerable explosion blew the top of the wireless set to pieces. Bits of wireless set and 20 mm shrapnel flew across the cabin and Campbell, the wireless operator was slightly wounded in the arm but Dutch Holland, standing alongside, had a remarkable escape.

As we turned one bend of the river we had a moment's peace. Only one searchlight was on us and that was from dead astern. No longer blinded I lifted my head from the instrument panel to see the river below us and no guns firing. The searchlight beam was a large circle of light in the centre of which the shadow of our Hudson was completely outlined — wings, engines, fuselage and turret, rudders, and even the suggestion of the exhaust flames. It was a moment of considerable beauty but it was not to last for long; it was blotted out with brutal suddenness as another searchlight got on to us and we were back in the routine of being hammered from all sides by the multi-coloured streaks of light, all with hard centres.

I was feeling very sorry for us when Bill shouted and pointed through the roof again. 'God, more trouble,' I thought. But there, many thousands of feet above us, a group of searchlights had caught an aircraft, its silvery belly reflecting every particle of light and betraying it as one of our Hudsons. It was surrounded by exploding shells and seemed in a very tight spot indeed. 'Thank God,' I thought uncharitably, 'that someone else is getting a load of sherbet flung at them, too,' and got on with the business of conducting our own affairs, which weren't going at all well.

'Gluckstadt ahead,' cried Bill, just to encourage me. Another naval base and more guns to contend with. They lived up to their expected reputation and took over the job of plastering us with multi-coloured projectiles while keeping us illuminated like a gigantic moth. We fled further up-river and left the hellish place behind but others took up the torch, so to speak, so there was little to choose between them. Crash after crash, the shots kept hitting us and, surely, it could only be a matter of time, a very short time in view of the intensity of hits, before we received our *coup de grace.* There was a moment of light relief, however as the Elbe became narrower and streams of tracer came at us from both sides of the river and two guns, one on each bank, did a really good traverse on us but used just that little bit too much deflection. I gazed unhappily at the death-laden streaks of light 20 yards in front of the nose, ready to ram the stick forward and dive the moment they showed the slightest sign of coming closer, but they dipped obligingly underneath us and I spared the time to wonder at the pattern the tracer made as it bounced and skidded off the roof tops to our right.

As we turned sharp right at the next bend in the river I looked back through the side window and saw two streams of tracer still criss-crossing the river but quite stationary. I felt sure that the north bank gunner had shot perilously close to the south bank gun position, or *vice versa,* and that the two guns were getting rid of their anger in a mutual shoot-out. The tracer crossed from side to side and skidded off the roof tops at all angles and they were still at it when I had to pay attention to more important matters. We had reached Altona and it was time to turn into the southern branch of the Elbe. After three more miles of the mixture as before we found our target area and turned off the river into the docks where the searchlights were, if anything, worse than ever.

We ran over the target at about 300 feet with the bomb doors open and I awaited Bill's welcome cry of 'Bombs gone,' but it didn't come. Bill came up the stairs out of the nose and said he couldn't see the target for searchlights and that we'd have to do another run. I glared unhappily at him and did it, and it wasn't all that easy. I could only take quick peeps at the ground or I became blinded myself; I flew much of the time with my head below window level and my face nearly touching the instrument panel and with Bill now down in the nose I hadn't his help in conning the aircraft. We came in for the second run and I felt pretty confident that I was on line but Bill appeared yet again, still blinded. We did a third run, during which an explosive shell hit the aircraft, but neither of us could really see, so we packed it in and brought the bombs away. You must remember that this was early days in the war. Area bombing, in other words, blasting every single thing that stood or moved, had not yet come into vogue. The Hun hadn't started to flatten our cities and the complete barbarism of blitzing hadn't yet arisen. A year later I'd have had no second thoughts about it, I would have pressed the 'Jettison' button on the second run if Bill hadn't dropped the bombs, and to hell with where they hit, but near the oil tanks was a hospital, well marked on the target map; we were peacetime trained to try and hit a specific target; and our job was reconnaissance in which we again aimed for accuracy. All our training was against loosing off a load of explosives haphazardly in a populated area.

I didn't return to the river. I'd seen enough of the Elbe to last me the rest of my life, which had every prospect of being a short one unless we could get away from the incessant gunfire and the periodic crashing of direct hits. I swung 90 degrees to the right and fled westwards into open country where a marvellous peace descended on us. We still kept low but there wasn't a gun or a searchlight in sight. We scraped perilously low over some high-tension power pylons so I took her up a bit for safety and then, as though to confound my decision to go higher, a gun opened up on us. My immediate reaction was rage that they couldn't leave us in peace even for five minutes, then I saw some aircraft hangers sweep by underneath; we were over an aerodrome. With the bomb doors opening we came round in a steep turn and gave them the four two-fifties in the hangars, and I remember thinking that the resulting explosion wasn't quite what one expects from such a load.

Crossing the coast south of Cuxhaven some sporadic anti-aircraft stuff came up at us and then we were out into the peace of the North Sea and went up to 2,000 feet to cruise comfortably along on autopilot. Apart from the loss of the wireless set we seemed in adequate shape and we made an accurate landfall and flew on to North Coates. We came in on the paraffin flarepath, the floodlight came on and I did a gentle wheeler on to the grass. The first gooseneck flare went by under the port wing, then the second and then the tail sank to the ground and they switched off the floodlight. But the third flare did not appear where it should have been. It seemed to be tracking right into the wing root. After it disappeared no more flares appeared and, in the darkness, I became aware of a horrible swing to port and of the shuddering of the undercarriage under some pretty brutal treatment. With full opposite brake and rudder we slewed round, jarring, creaking and banging to a harsh final judder as she stopped in the pitch-black morning. We came to rest pointing more or less back the way we'd come. We'd got a flat port tyre. Again.

We got out and stood in the cold, waiting to be collected. There was a heavy dew on the grass and we'd skidded more easily than at Lossiemouth a month before, and more extensively as the skid had really developed by the time I'd cottoned on to it in the dark. We left her out on the grass and de-briefed in the Ops Room. It was a flat sort of business. The Intelligence Officer found us a nuisance as the attack didn't fit in with the sort of report he was used to putting in.

'You say you went in three times over the target at 300 feet yet didn't drop your bombs on it. Why?'

'Well, you see, there was an awful lot of glare; we couldn't really see it.'

'But you say you went right over it each time. How can you make such a statement if you couldn't see?'

'Well, we got our line from the dock wall but we didn't know precisely when we were over the tanks.'

'And you didn't drop your bombs?'

'No, at least not then. Hospitals and things, you know.'

He sighed, marked the form 'Target not attacked' and we drifted off to the rather crummy beds that had been dragged together for the visiting team.

We caught a few hours' sleep and I hung around while Bill and Dutch tucked into their aircrew breakfast of bacon and eggs, then all three of us walked the half mile across the aerodrome to where we'd abandoned N7340 in the cold at 3.30 that morning. Even from a distance you could see that the wing had already been jacked up to replace the wheel with the burst tyre.

"You've got to hand it to Flight Sergeant Radlett," said Dutch, "He's an insubordinate sod but, by God, he gets things done."

Radlett was 'B' Flight's servicing N.C.O. and he came to meet us as we approached. Never one to be impressed by junior officers, he let us all know that it was only with the greatest reluctance that he handed over his aircraft for us to fly. His vocabulary of adjectives was limited to two, and he overworked them both. He opened the batting.

"That's a fine bloody mess you've made of my effing aircraft," he said.

"Not me, Chiefy,"[1] I said, "*I* didn't shoot those holes in it; it was those trigger-happy goons across the drink."

"Yes, but if you'd had the sense to do what the rest of the effing squadron did and flown at 12,000 effing feet instead of arsing around at two hundred it would have looked more like an effing aircraft and less like a bloody colander. How the hell am I going to get this thing airworthy this side of Xmas?" "Sir," he added belatedly.

"Oh, thank you so much, Flight Sergeant," I said.

"What for?"

"That 'Sir', Chiefy. Don't get many of them from you, do I?"

"Well, if you treat my effing aircraft like this you won't get many bloody more, either." "Sir."

He was obviously relenting.

Bill stepped in before he got going again.

"Look, Chiefy," he said, "Will she fly? I don't know about you but I want to get home."

"Well, you've no bloody wireless, of course, some clown has

[1]Flight Sergeants were often called 'Chiefy'.

shot the shit out of it, but we've a real problem with the elevator. I'll get a torch."

We went round to the tail, where the 20 mil had blown a hole about 6 inches in diameter in the top surface of the elevator.

"That's no problem, Chiefy."

"No, but have a look inside — the elevator bell crank."

He shone his torch into the hole and the reason for his concern became apparent; a shell splinter had clipped about a third of the metal out of one of the arms of the bell crank. Whatever load the metal was designed for, it now possessed only two-thirds of the capability to carry and, of the three basic control surfaces, the elevator was far and away the most important. If control of that was lost at low altitude we were dead men. We held a conference.

"It's your decision, Sir," said Flight Sergeant Radlett.

"Point taken, Chiefy. How long would it take to get and fit a new one?"

"Depends on how soon we can get the first aircraft away to Leuchars, get the effing spare and fly back here. Then a full day to fit it. With luck, two more days." I thought of the crummy, cold wooden hut we'd slept in, the fact that it didn't seem like home, the unfamiliar faces, the unappreciative Intelligence Officer who was quite obviously bored and unimpressed with our lack of attack on the main target. I didn't feel like two more days at North Coates.

Bill helped me out.

"Well," he said, "We've come all the way from Hamburg without dropping to bits. That damage must have been done over the target and you've horsed the aircraft round a fair bit since then. I vote we fly."

As we spoke an armourer sidled up to me and said 'Could I have a word with you, Sir?" I left Bill and the Flight Sergeant poking away at the elevator and followed him under the aircraft. As I looked up into the bomb bay I knew why I was there.

"Oh, shit," I said disappointedly. Hanging from one of the bomb racks was the fusing link of a two-fifty pounder. But only one. There should have been four!

Three of the four bombs which we'd dropped on that aerodrome had fallen away 'Safe', and wouldn't have exploded. I'd thought at the time that, considering we were only at a couple of hundred feet, there hadn't been all that much of a guffufle when they went off but my mind had been on other things, like avoiding the power cables that we'd only just cleared as we'd turned back to drop our bombs. The initial inference was that Bill had forgotten to select the fusing switches of those bombs, but this was unlikely as he'd certainly fused *one* of them.

"Go into the cockpit, Chambers, put the Master and bomb circuit switches on and flip each fusing switch on and off three times."

After a pause the fusing box which held the solitary fusing link clicked three times. Apart from that there was silence, until I heard the armourer's feet clumping down the cabin floor above me. One didn't have to look twice at the half dozen bullet holes in the bomb doors to know what had happened — three of the four fusing circuits had been shot through by gunfire. It was very disappointing; all that effort for one single bomb, and that not on the primary target, either. The single consolation was that the fact that the Hun would have to declare the place where the three unexploded bombs had fallen a no-go area for a day or two to ensure that they had not got long-delay fuses and then a day or two to dig them out. I hoped that they would have as much difficulty getting them out as we'd had delivering them. I felt a bit depressed.

L.A.C. Campbell, the wireless operator, appeared with his arm in a sling.

"Hello, Campbell, what's the extent of the damage? Anything serious?"

"I've had a few bits of the wireless set blown into my upper arm and some small nerves have been cut. Three of my fingers don't work very well but the M.O. says he's taken all the bits out and that it should resolve in a week or two."

"Well, you haven't got a set to work anyway, so you can have a sleep on the way home. We should be off within the hour."

By 11.20 we were airborne and heading northwards for Leuchars. The feeling of depression deepened.

It was Bill's turn to fly and mine to navigate, which was a matter of reading a newspaper in the nose and letting Bill do a coast-crawl. It was a rather silent aircraft that wended its way northwards. It had been an experience that we were lucky to survive and we all knew it. I felt depressed by the failure of my bright idea, at our helplessness in the face of such an overwhelming amount of light and gunfire and at the final blow of the shot-through fusing circuits, meaning that only one bomb had gone off. Maybe I was a pretty bum captain. I certainly had a pretty bum aircraft. The slipstream shrieked across the numerous bullet holes, there were cracked and broken windows, 20 mm holes in wings and elevators and a torrent of cold air poured into the cabin through the hole where the 20 mil had wrecked the wireless set. Were *all* my ideas bad, I wondered?

To help disperse my depression I suggested a bit of low flying to Bill, but he just wasn't interested. A grunted negative came down the phones. I felt bloody-minded and taunted him but he wouldn't do it and, after all, he was doing the flying so I went back to my paper and we flew silently on. We crossed the Firth of Forth and, now that Bill was back on home ground, it looked as though the old spark was returning as we were losing height. I stuffed my paper in the map rack and watched the shoreline come closer. Then we were speeding along the cliff top at St. Andrews and the Grand Hotel, that haunt of aircrew, came in sight and the old Bill arose like a phoenix in the cockpit. The engines went to full throttle, we went down to a few feet off the cliff top and he flung the Hudson into a vertical turn that shoved her belly almost against the side of the hotel. Alas, no one on earth can hold height in a vertical turn in a bomber and the inevitable happened. A bit on the late side Bill put on full opposite aileron and hauled back on the elevator but, with the aircraft straightening out and still pointing upwards, she sank firmly earthwards across the roof of the Royal and Ancient Golf Club and towards the beach. I looked between my feet through the transparent bombing panel as first the pebbles, then the individual grains of sand, came rapidly into focus. 'Christ, he's really lost it this time,' I thought, and waited peacefully for death as we slammed into the ground.

It didn't come. We hit a ground effect[1] in a way I'd never hit it before or ever hope to again. We could feel that enormous cushion of air doing its utmost to shove nine tons of aircraft back into the air where it belonged. A large swirl of sand spun up from where the port propeller tips flailed only inches from the ground, rattled noisily against the underside of the wing and was lost as we sailed upwards into normal flight. Nobody said a thing. In deafening silence we climbed away and joined the circuit at Leuchars. Heaven knows what the crew thought of their two pilots. Twice in two days we'd nearly copped a packet. And Bill had obviously completely forgotten about the shot-through elevator bell crank that he'd just been hauling on with all his might.

Bill wheeled her on to the runway and a thoughtful crew, older and wiser in years than when they'd left Leuchars 27 hours before, got out on to the tarmac. Bill made a gallant face-saving

[1]Ground effect — As the aircraft nears the ground, as in landing, the air between the ground and the lower surface of the wing gets 'squeezed' into the relatively confined space. This provides extra lift and causes the aircraft to float a bit.

effort. 'Listen, Dopey,' he said, poking me in the chest with his forefinger (a habit I deplore), 'The next time we get a flat *I'm* going to be the one to land the aircraft, get it?'

Ever one for the peaceful life, I agreed, but we never did the hat trick so just how good Bill was at burst-tyre landings I never knew.

We went up to the Ops Room to go over the raid again with our own Intelligence Officer and walked back to the Mess with others of the Hamburg team. Some of them had received a fair amount of damage from the heavy ack-ack (two wounded crew members had been left behind in hospital at North Coates) and they were full of it. As I've stated earlier, heavy ack-ack from ships didn't worry us all that much as it was so delightfully inaccurate and, although the occasional aircraft fell foul of it, this was more through bad luck than through good shooting on the Hun's part. Even the harbour installations at places like Bergen and Kristiansand weren't too bad so long as you got in quickly and shot off like a scalded cat after you'd dropped your load. The stuff that (literally) got us down was the light flak — the rifle-calibre machine-guns and 20 and 40 mm automatics, which hose-piped hundreds of rounds at you at close range as you did your low level bombing attack or reconnaissance. However, it looked as though the mainland of Germany was quite another matter. We'd seen the Whitley and our Hudson caught by searchlights and getting plastered and we didn't need any convincing that the boys up top had had their harassing moments, but it was a bit annoying to find that the high-level brigade dismissed our low-flying episode so perfunctorily. They chattered like monkeys about seeing the smoke of the bursting shells as well as the flashes.

'I thought there was one-tenth cloud at 12,000 feet,' said one. 'I could see it drifting through the exhaust flames. Then I realised it was smoke from the shell bursts. Jesus! You could nearly walk on the stuff! You should have seen it, Dopey!'

'Well, I did. From a distance, so to speak. We did have the odd spot of trouble down at ground level, mind you. Light flak and all that sort of thing.'

'Yeeees. Well, you could expect that down there, couldn't you? I mean, we all know about that, don't we? Get it every day of the week in this job. But you should have seen *this* stuff. They fired more shells at me than you've had hot dinners.'

Someone else chimed in and it seemed pretty pointless trying to put my point. There was only one topic of conversation — heavy ack-ack. Bill and I mumbled away to each other; at least we each had someone who would understand. We *really* had had the shit shot out of us last night. As we went in through the Mess doors the conversation ceased temporarily and I seized my chance as we all streamed into the ante-room for a swift pint.

'If you buggers think you've had a hard time just go down to B Flight workshops and have a look at poor old N7340. She looks like a bloody colander'.

'Agreed, old boy, but I still say . . .' His voice trailed away to nothing. Something strange was happening. Around the radiogram in the corner was a large group of aircrew, all their faces turned towards us, and every face with a hostile expression on it. One face appeared to be bellowing.

'What on earth's up?' said one of the Hamburg team.

'For thc *Third* time will you all bloody well shut up,' bellowed the face.

'What have we done wrong?' queried another puzzled character. 'Apart, that is, from risking our bacon over Hamburg while you lot sat on your arses in comfort?'

'Shut up! Bloody well shut up!' bellowed all the faces in unison.

'Welcome home!' muttered Bill sarcastically and, as we all shut up, we became conscious of the heinousness of our crime. The squadron song was on.

At almost full volume the plaintive and arresting voice of Vera Lynn singing *'It's a Lovely Day Tomorrow'* was coming over the radio. In spellbound silence the Mess listened and forgot the war. As the song finished the silence continued for many seconds. Then the adjutant slowly got to his feet.

'Ah, back from Hamburg, I see,' he said. 'Any casualties? Have you all got back safely?'

We assured him that, apart from the two left behind at North Coates, and my wireless operator, all was well.

'Jolly good,' he said. 'First rate. We were a bit worried about you. Thought it might be a bit dodgy, you know, and we're very glad to see you all again. But, er, next time you come in when Vera Lynn's singing 'It's a Lovely day Tomorrow' don't make so much bloody noise.'

It was an unnecessary request. Had we known it was on we would have streaked from the Ops Room in double-quick time and flowed silently into the mess to drink in that haunting melody and the voice of 'The Forces' Sweetheart.' Which was a bit of cheek on the part of the rest of the forces. She was really 233 Squadron's property and the song our song.

I sang it dozens of times on my trips to Norway. Our job allowed plenty of time for thinking, and singing if you felt like it, chiefly when on the way home and well away from the dangers of the Norwegian coast. When the pressure was off both the pilot's and the navigator's seats of a Hudson were great places for philosophy. Earthly worries such as income tax and your low rate of pay tended to be replaced by more sublime thoughts; you could set the world to rights as you went through the automatic routine of running an engine check or taking a glance at the white horses on the sea below to note any change in wind direction.

But I was becoming increasingly aware that recently the trend of my philosophising was away from the lofty and was now much concerned with the practical matter of survival. As the Norwegian campaign went on our casualties continued to mount. At increasingly shorter intervals machine after machine failed to return from patrol. Though the actual cause would be unknown it was chiefly the overwhelming superiority, in numbers, armament and performance, of the Messerschmitt 109 fighter. But it could be flak when attacking shipping, an occasional unlucky shot when fighting an aircraft of similar performance such as the Junkers 88 or just bad weather. But you never knew just *what* it was. About seven and a half hours after the machine took off, if it had not returned and had sent no diversion signal, the anxiety started, both among the flying crews in the Flight Offices and the ground crew awaiting the return of their aircraft. The occasional lone figure would be seen walking out onto the aerodrome and looking eastward, listening attentively for the growing sound of Cyclone engines, then giving up and walking quietly back. An hour later the Flight Sergeant would send the ground crew off to their quarters and a silence would descend on the Flight Office as each person quietly mourned the loss of friends, and gave five per cent of their time to wondering if it was going to be them next time. The casualties were normally of single aircraft at a time, because the majority of our work was done individually, but we had the occasional disaster, as when a flight of three aircraft just vanished into the blue. If we were detailed for a specific attack on a well-defended target such as a major naval unit then we expected casualties, and the unlucky aircraft were often seen going down by others of the attacking force, so that we knew their fate; but the uncertainty attached to the 'Failed to Return' category somehow gave an added element of threat.

Bad weather, though entirely without the shot-and-shell glamour of air combat that thrilled the newspaper readers, was a very wearing business that also sometimes led to deaths, such as Tinker Bell's in Norway before the war had even started, and Mike Clarke's when almost safely home. When the clouds were low and rain and sleet reduced the visibility to only hundreds of yards you had to balance the importance of the job against the fact that it was now getting dangerous to fly; and you went deeper and deeper into the murk hoping that it *might* get better if you carried on just that little bit further. You often ended up squeezed into a couple of hundred feet of airspace between the grey wispiness of the lowest part of the cloudbase and the heaving desolation of the North Sea below, which would smash you into scrap metal if you hit it. At this stage you usually took out the automatic pilot and flew manually, and then the strain started in earnest. If you once lost sight of the sea in a wisp of cloud then you had immediately to pull up into the overcast with no hope of getting down through it again, and you climbed, hoping to break out of it in due course and that it would eventually clear enough to give you a safe landing back home. The belt of Scottish hills that lay inland at varying distances from the coast made flying low when lost in cloud a dodgy business. While we could use wireless when in trouble, traffic was always kept to a minimum so as to give the enemy as little information on our movements as possible, and you didn't want to start bleating the moment you started getting a bit unhappy. In any case all we could get in the way of assistance was a bearing or a fix; we had no instrument landing system for the all-important final approach and touch-down, and it was at this stage of the flight, when so near home, that many aircraft and crews met their end.

Although it had not been one of ours, a Blenheim had slammed mysteriously into the ground just off the aerodrome. On a pig of a day, with the cloud base ten-tenths at about 200 feet, we were all snugged up safely in the Mess when some of us heard a noise like the slamming of a car door. Only those of us who'd heard it before knew that it wasn't. We had no aircraft flying but the phones started to ring and we eventually found, in a ploughed field only 200 yards from the edge of the aerodrome, what looked like a miniature moonscape — a large, elongated hole in the ground with boulder-like clumps of tough clay thrown up round the edge like a jagged rampart. From the centre of this riven mess protruded a few crumpled feet of the tail end of a Blenheim. The rest was six feet in. The aircraft had gone in vertically and this was another of those accidents where one didn't have to delve into the wreckage to try to save life. The three crew were six feet down in that awful mass of metal and earth and we could leave it now to the engineering and medical departments and get back to our newspapers. I never knew their names, except for a few hours when I was one of those detailed to attend the funeral, but I felt that it was a bleak way to die, so near to an RAF aerodrome and yet so far from their own squadron that we didn't know who they were.

The two flying accidents that had affected me most were those of Robinson and Godfrey on the second day of the war, when we had to wade and slither through mud and fire-fighting foam to get their bodies out of the flaming wreck and that of the 224 Squadron Hudson that had spun into the ground only a few hundred yards away from me when I was out on a walk. I hadn't bothered to go to *that* crash as it was obvious the crew hadn't a hope; I carried on with my walk as I watched the greasy black smoke rise from behind the trees. And I imagine that the biggest single incident that had reduced my morale was my own crash into the estuary in October. Although I was then unaware of it, I don't suppose that concussion or amnesia helps all that much, and the frightful shock and dreadful ball of flame that were my last memories of the crash still haunted me, and the one person that I could have discussed it with, my second pilot, Sgt Hallam, had himself been killed a few weeks later in bad weather in South Wales.

Whatever casualties we had, although I missed the old faces that would appear no more, I found that the new faces that replaced them caused me as much trouble. There seemed to be so many of them and I never quite seemed to catch up with getting to know them all. It wasn't that I was developing into a crusty old timer; at 21 I was capable of rapid adjustment, but I shrank into a smaller circle of companionship. Along with most of the squadron I was beginning to feel that life was becoming without hope. So long as hope exists you can seize on to it, because each of you feels privately that it will never really happen to you; it will be the other chap who actually gets the chop. But there was no established 'Operational Tour' for aircrew, the '30 trip' bomber tour hadn't been invented. We were Regular Air Force, we were short of crews and aircraft, so we just went on, as far as we could estimate, until we died. None of us ever mentioned it to anyone else; it was never a topic of conversation but, as we had a degree of intelligence, it was obvious to us all that that was going to be the normal course of events. Admittedly we now had twelve days' leave each three months but you knew that, at the end of it, you had to come back.

And a twist of fate was that, at a well-established peace-time station like Leuchars, the good social life and home comforts extended by the local people were, in actual fact, doing us all a disservice although we didn't know it. The contrast between being shot at by the Hun and, five hours later, of sitting in a comfortable drawing room literally eating cucumber sandwiches and discussing the church bazaar was quite unnatural. It was too much of a mental shuttle. I remember, during a 48-hour stand-down which I spent in Joan's parents' comfortable house in St. Andrews, being rung up by the Despatching Officer who apologised for bursting in on me but I'd have to come back immediately to fly as we were short of a pilot. I remember protesting, and then finally arguing with him until, in exasperation, he rasped 'For Christ's sake Dopey, shut up and come back and fly this bloody aeroplane. I'm sending transport for you. See that you're ready for it.' As he slammed the phone down I felt quite ashamed of my protest but still felt deep resentment that the war could invade this comfortable house and snatch me out of it. If I'd been off-duty in the Mess I wouldn't have bitched in the slightest; the odd wry comment on the Despatching Officer's parentage, perhaps, but nothing else.

Mind you, I'd been finding recently that even cucumber sandwiches weren't all that they'd been cracked up to be. For some time I'd been aware of an almost perpetual feeling of hunger that made me want to eat, and of the incomprehensible abolition of that hunger with almost the first mouthful of the eagerly awaited meal. This was followed by an acid, burning feeling in my stomach that became quite painful for an hour or more at a time. Apart from this, in the background, I had a dragging, leaden feeling in my stomach as though I had a cannon ball in it. The cannon ball was a fairly constant companion about which it appeared I could do little, but I felt that intelligence could deal with the other matter. If I had hunger pangs which were so easily abolished by a few mouthfuls of food then it was obvious that I was eating too much. I experimented by cutting out first one, then two meals and fell ravenously on the single meal of the day, to be reduced to impotent anger and disappointment as the hunger so rapidly vanished, only to be replaced by the acid burning in my gut and I left the table, defeated once more.

I decided I'd beat the thing and went a whole day without food, sweeping into breakfast the next morning with the appetite of a horse and claiming my 'aircrew breakfast' of bacon and egg, now fast becoming a luxury. About one rasher and half the egg later I only half heard the comment of the Equipment Officer as I left the table: 'For God's sake, Dopey, if you don't want the food why start on it? You might as well give it away.'

Which was a bit maddening as I already *was*. Although I drew my flying ration of sandwiches I had already given up nibbling at them and gave them away to Tubby Davies, my wireless operator. I'd never know Tubby refuse grub and he laid into it in a manner that I viewed half with envy and half with resentment. There was only one bonus. Several of the elder members of my family ran to fat and I'd always had a horror of it, so much so that, at about the age of fourteen, I'd answered an advertisement in a women's paper for a free sample of a slimming pill. Unfortunately I didn't intercept the postman in time and the small parcel, addressed to *Miss* G. Edwards was, of course, handed to my sister of similar initial.

'Dear Madam,' the letter informed the mystified nine-year-old, 'in response to your request I enclose a free sample of our Super Fairylight weight-reducing compound . . . '

My mother expounded wrathfully on the lengths to which unprincipled manufacturers were prepared to take the hard sell and flung the packet in the bin, so I never found out how effective it was.

So, what had once been a time of philosophy in the cockpit was, almost inevitably, becoming more and more a time for brooding. I suppose that it was the hopelessness of our situation that really got us down — the lack of any let-up in the routine of crashed and missing aircraft — and many of us were becoming silent and depressed. As we were driven out to our dispersed aircraft by Crasher in her 15 cwt Bedford, we found that the jolly back-chat of the cinema flier had more or less vanished on the outward trip. It was a bit different on the return trip, of course. A relieved bunch of guys gave her her share of leg-pulling; after all, they'd probably got a day or two's freedom from worry before the next patrol. And, in one's more reasonable moments, one had to admit that a big bonus in bad weather was the virtual certainty of complete safety from 109s. The low visibility rendered the chance of fighter interception negligible: if they did see us they'd be too busy trying not to hit the sea themselves to concentrate on firing at the same time, but, even if they tried it, a quick backward pressure on the control column had you safely up in the clouds in a couple of seconds. Although you then had the more prolonged, gnawing anxiety of having to get out of the cloud and in sight of the ground before you were safe again, but it was infinitely preferable to being shot up by an aircraft a hundred miles an hour faster than you were, and with about twenty times the firepower.

A strange feature of my pre-flight brooding was its abolition as soon as I got the engines started. As Crasher stopped her Bedford at the aircraft we tumbled out, grunted some sort of farewell to the other crews and climbed fairly silently aboard. The drag of the cannon ball in my stomach increased as I settled into the seat, strapped in, received the reports of the fitter, rigger and armourer and went into the engine-starting routine. With the side window open one shouted to the world at large the excellent advice 'Stand clear of the airscrews', followed by 'Contact port' and one pressed the starter and booster buttons. The port airscrew would grind into motion, slowly and jerkily at first, then with increasing speed and smoothness and, as one threw the magneto switches to 'Contact', the Cyclone engine would fire into life with its characteristic throaty gobbling.

As soon as this happened there was an immediate lightening of spirit and the feeling of dread and oppression vanished as I prepared to enter the air, the element in which I felt completely at home. It was like putting on an old coat: well known, comfortable and secure. On equal terms I was as good as anybody else in the air. I mean, how many other pilots did I know who could produce that 'Exceptional' assessment from their Flying Training Schools? I hadn't met one yet! But this sense of relief was a bit unintelligent when you think about it. If I hadn't had to fly I wouldn't have felt morose anyway.

Not all that dramatic, but the cause of many a destroyed-by-fire Hudson. If the rivetting of the skin of the port wing had given way the petrol would have poured out. The muzzle of the right-hand fixed Browning gun can be seen protruding above the navigator's compartment in the nose. (Group Captain Roy Fuller).

Not again! 223 Squadron's Demolition Unit. This transformer was demolished by McLaven late in 1939, his Hudson being destroyed in the accident. Troughten-Smith and Piejus had another, equally-successful, go at it in 1940 and, incredibly, walked away.
The score when I left the squadron in 1940 was still Hudsons 2, Transformers 2.
(Group Captain Roy Fuller)

10 May 1940. HMS 'Kelly', Lord Louis Mountbatten's flotilla leader, torpedoed off Jutland by an E-Boat. Ship shown listing with her starboard rail under water. Note crew standing on the port side and the topmasts of an accompanying destroyer behind the bridge. 'Kelly' was towed home and repaired, being finally sunk off Crete in 1941. (The Photo Source)

Lord Louis Mountbatten, Supreme Commander, South-East Asia, talking to the author about the torpedoing of HMS 'Kelly' in 1940.

22 June 1940. A Dornier 18K flying boat of the type which we found shadowing the naval forces which we were escorting. We ended up in a cloud shooting it out at about 20 yards range.

Gunner of a Dornier 18K. Similar to the view I had of the front gunner, a shadowy sinister fellow but, in my case, the gun was pointing directly at me. Rather daunting.

The two aircraft which caused us the most concern, and which undoubtedly were responsible for the majority of our casualties, were the Messerschmitt 109 and 110. Both aircraft were greatly superior to our Hudsons in performance and armament. They also had the advantages of fighting close to home so that a higher proportion of damaged aircraft would return to base. After an encounter with one of these we could be faced with a 350-mile journey and there is no doubt that many aircraft did not survive such a trip.

The 109E. Speed 354 m.p.h. (110 m.p.h. faster than we were), armament two 20 mm cannon, two rifle-calibre machine guns. At any one time we could only oppose it with two rifle-calibre machine guns. In any one second the 109 fired twelve times the weight of bullets that we could fire. (I.W.M.)

The 110. Speed 360 m.p.h. Carried two more machine guns than the 109. This is an example captured intact and flown in R.A.F. markings. The muzzles of two of the machine guns can be seen protruding from the nose. (I.W.M.)

Chapter 6

Bill was on leave, despite which they hadn't stopped the war or anything and I did a few trips with some of the newly-arrived replacements for our more recent casualties. On the day that Belgium surrendered my navigator was to be Paton and we checked into the Operations Room, seeking out Corporal Davies and Leading Aircraftman Morgan, our wireless operator and air gunner.

'Regular bunch of Celts, aren't we?' I observed, 'Three Taffies and a Scot. Hope you don't feel too outnumbered, Paton. Where d'you come from.?'

'Small village. You won't have heard of it. Tomintoul.'

'Aha! Highest village in Scotland, they tell me,' I observed brightly.

'No, not that one, the other one. Near Braemar.'

'Oh. Didn't know there could be two with a name like that. Nearly as bad as *my* home village, Rhydymwyn.

'Silence please, gentlemen,' called the Ops Room Controller. 'Now we think that a self-contained raiding unit of the German Navy is going to break out soon as they've left Brunsbuttel and have obviously gone through the Keil canal into the Baltic. They should appear in the Norwegian fiords for their final break-out. Two cruisers and their supply ships. The cruisers will get out fast and the supply ships will probably go independently at the best speed they can make, making full use of the hours of darkness, of course. Six aircraft, four from 233 and two from 224 will do a parallel track search twenty miles apart to hit the coast between Bergen and Stavanger and will return on tracks 10 miles to the south after searching the fiords at the ends of their landfalls. Navigators are to collect their departure, search and return times from the Navigation Officer. Out on a track of 040 degrees, back on 220 degrees.

Now, as to tactics, reconnaissance is paramount; attack, though desirable, secondary. If you can get a quick signal off we might get a strike force off from here and 269 Squadron at Wick, and perhaps some mine-laying Hampdens as well. When your signal has been acknowledged then you can attack. You will carry semi-armour piercing bombs in case you meet the cruisers.

Now it would be nice it you could all gang up and attack as a unit of six but I wouldn't advise you to do it. That coast is swarming with Messerschmitt 109s and in the half-hour it would take you to assemble they'd be on to you like a ton of bricks. By the time you get off your signal the ships will be alerted and waiting for you anyway, so don't push your luck too far. Attack and get the hell out of it. Good Hunting!'

Paton went off to see the Navigation Officer while I nattered to the other five pilots. He returned looking a bit harrassed.

'Look,' he said, 'I'm just about going round the bend about timings. I don't get it. All six aircraft set off at different departure times from Scotland, have different search times in Norway and set off for home at different times. Fred Karno hasn't organised this sweep, has he?'

'No, it's all quite logical. Look, we've got a bit of time, come over here in the corner and I'll explain.'

I drew the following diagram:-

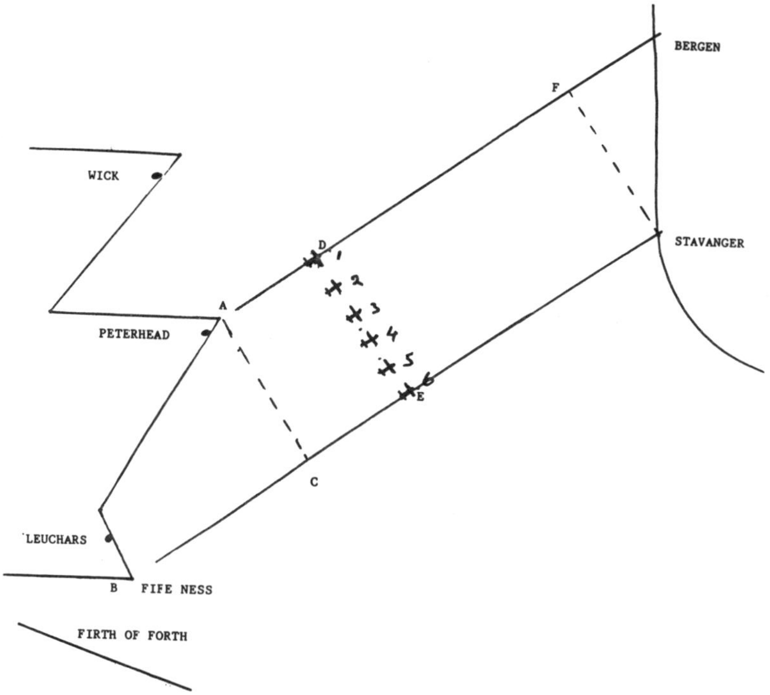

We want the six aircraft to go out in line abreast as in DE. Now aircraft No. 1 has the longest distance to fly to his departure point at A and No. 6 one of the shortest. But No. 6 then has to fly from Fife Ness to be at C at the same time as as No. 1 leaves Peterhead. At the end of the patrol No. 6 arrives in Norway first, at Stavanger, while the others have to fly on varying distances, No. 1 having the furthest to go, from F to Bergen. No. 6 will be allotted the greatest reconnaissance time and No. 1 the shortest as, not only has he to fly the furthest distance on to Norway but has also to fly a similar distance back to F, or ten miles south of it actually. In view of the extent of the fiord system it appears odd to give different search times to each aircraft but the most important aspect is the efficiency of the sea sweep, which is best accomplished in line abreast. So we can't give everyone as much time hunting the fiords as we would like. I wouldn't mind betting that a second operation is already being planned which does the reverse, depending on what *we* find, with the accent on just getting aircraft over there to do a more extensive search of the waterways. You needn't worry about anything except our own departure points and times, and keeping an accurate track — regular checks on our drift. Later on you could end up as Squadron Navigation Officer, in which case you'd have to plan this sort of thing, but that's all in the future, forget about it now. (Sadly, Paton never did become Navigation Officer. Within two months he'd joined the ranks of those who 'Failed to Return').

'Look, tell you what. I'll navigate and you fly but, if anything urgent turns up, like those ships we're after or a gaggle of 109s, I want you out of that seat in two shakes of a lamb's tail and I'll take over. On the way out have a good think about how the whole patrol's been organised, but don't let it distract your attention from keeping a good lookout.'

We flew north to our departure from Buddon Ness and set off on our track of 040 degrees. As soon as we'd settled down on course I went down the stairs into the navigator's compartment in the nose, slid my seat forward on its runners and lay down to take a drift with the bombsight through the transparent floor panel, using one of the larger white horses of spray on the sea's surface as a mark. By general size of these white horses the wind speed was a bit over what the met forecast had given and our drift was 4 degrees more to starboard than I'd reckoned. Uncorrected, that would have given us an error of 25 miles in our landfall. I switched on my intercomm.

'Alter course 4 degrees port on to 042 degrees magnetic,' I told Paton.

'Oh four two magnetic it is, Dopey. Testing guns.'

There were two *clunks* from the Browning guns mounted two feet above my head as Paton pulled the gun loading handles. As I looked up at the right-hand gun the cocking handle vanished into a blur as both guns banged and rattled into action at twenty shots a second apiece. Spent cases and links tinkled down into the empties bags and cordite fumes leaked and swirled round my compartment. The aircraft yawed; that would be Morgan swinging his turret on to the beam to do a test firing of *his* guns. Faintly, above the engine and slipstream noise, a muted rat-tat-tat confirmed this.

I settled down to ten minutes of forward planning. Using the amended groundspeed derived from my drift checks I marked off along our track line my estimated position at ten minute intervals so that if anything turned up suddenly I would have a fair idea of its position immediately, and could leave the accurate estimation until an opportunity to work it out presented itself. It could save precious seconds in one's preliminary sighting report. The Hudson settled down on its patrol, Paton would be sweeping the horizon forward from wing tip to wing tip and Morgan in the turrett would be doing the same astern, their sideways sweeps overlapping each beam. Paton would probably be the first to spot anything, and he had a pair of binoculars available for confirming any suspicious sighting. As navigator I would be reinforcing his search forward through the transparent nose, when I wasn't occupied on my own chores, though navigators often came up the stairs and stood or sat alongside the pilot in companionable silence, or to pass the time of day. There was a better view up top as the engines blanketed a lot of the lateral vision from the navigator's seat.

'How's the petrol consumption?' I asked on one of my trips upstairs, and gave Paton full marks for his answer.

'About 75 gallons in the first hour,' he replied. 'Just about right. We should be cruising at 67 gallons an hour and probably used that 8 gallons extra in take-off and climb-away. The cylinder-head temperatures are in the green so I can lean out the mixtures a bit more, if you like.'

'No. 67 gallons an hour will do. Don't want to run the engines too hot; it shouldn't be all that long a trip so I don't think we need to conserve fuel at the expense of engine wear.'

We saw nothing on the way over so ran into the mouth of Boknafiord and started our hunt for hiding ships.

'Now keep below the level of the tops of the mountains as much as you can,' I told Paton. 'They will have got us on their radar on our approach over the sea so they know we're here, but there's no point in making it easy for them. Stick below mountain level and their radar's useless. It'll be luck if their fighters find us as it'll be all eyeball stuff for them. If we have to go over a mountain range to get into the next fiord do a daisy-cutter across the top of it but be prepared for a good bump in a fresh wind like this one. There'll be a lot of turbulence around the tops, and a good number of downdraughts which you *must* be prepared for. If you get into a dodgy downdraught use every bit of throttle you have — right up to the gate, yank the levers sideways and shove them through to the stops. And you'll need all your physical strength occasionally, too; really *haul* on the controls if you have to. Just don't hit those mountains or the side of a fiord, they're damned hard.' We flitted up and down the tortuous waterways and I told Paton to nip over into the next fiord. 'Now, not *too* low over the top as you've not done it before. Are you strapped in really tight? No, leave it to me, I'll do it. You just fly.'

I yanked at his safety harness straps until they'd move no more and got a good hold of the bulkhead.

'We're going just about down wind so there's bound to be a down current the other side of the ridge, so not too low, mind you,' I shouted to Paton. 'Not below 150 feet off the top.' The Hudson shook and buffeted in the turbulence as we went over and I felt my stomach rise as we sank rapidly into the expected downdraught the other side. Paton anticipated adequately and we slid down the mountain into the next branch fiord

'Nicely done, old boy,' I told him. 'But don't forget, in really turbulent conditions you've got to watch things like a hawk. And *never* go so far up a fiord that you can't do a one-eighty[1] with plenty of spare room to get out in. If you go right to the top of some of these beauties you'd find yourself unable to climb out through the downdraughts and unable to turn round. You'd just take your crew right into the rock.'

There were no ships in this section of the fiord either and the time limit for our rejoining the sweep was approaching.

'O.K. Paton, that's it. Now we'll just take a slight risk and take her up above mountain height. We'll get as good a view of the rest of the waterways as we can and then go home.' But, even from our vantage point, we could not see any sign of a ship, either naval or auxiliary so we dived down to a safe height and I gave Paton the course for our departure point, which we should reach

[1]One-eighty. A 180-degree turn; right back on one's track.

in just over seven minutes.

'O.K., Paton,' I said, 'Do a complete intrument and fuel check and set her up for cruising.'

He'd just started on his chore when the intercomm came to life as L.A.C. Morgan cried 'Gunner to captain. Four 109s five miles astern.'

I heard the rattle as he test-fired his guns and I shouted 'Out of it, Paton. Quickly please.'

As Paton flung off his straps and scrambled out of the pilot's seat I slid in behind him. It took me about ten seconds to strap in, set the mixtures to rich, aircrews fully fine pitch and throttles to the gate.

'O.K. Morgan, got that. It'll be a minute or two before they catch up with us. Have a good look round to see if there are any more of them. I hope not or you might never sing *Sospan Fach* at Cardiff Arms Park again.

'Paton, get on the Lewis. Stick it out of the starboard window.'

Paton dashed off to the cabin and I felt the drafts rushing round the cockpit as he removed the two side windows through which we stuck our Lewis gun. As I pressed my gun button to test my own Brownings Paton opened up with the slower-firing Lewis gun, two short check bursts. We were as ready now as we ever would be.

'Captain to crew. They may not, of course, have seen us yet as we are fairly low. I'm going down on the deck now and turning out to sea. Paton, I'm turning on to our reciprocal six minutes early. We'll correct the navigation later.' I dived down to sea level, turned south-westwards and made a swift note on my knee pad of the time and compass course.

'How are the 109s Morgan? I asked the gunner.

'I think they're carrying on southwards, sir. They haven't turned out to sea yet.' I blessed the freshness of the wind that had given us that bumpy ride over the mountain tops. That same strong wind had churned the surface of the sea into a mass of white horses, the best camouflage there was. It would take a very keen eye to spot us fifty feet off the surface from three or four miles away. And the radar couldn't help the 109s at this height, either.

As we rushed towards our home 350 nautical miles away, an air of suspense pervaded the silent aircraft, silent because, as far as our alerted main senses went, the roar of the two thousand horsepower and the hiss of the slipstream were of no account. What we were waiting for was the gunner's next announcement, which seemed an age in coming. I nearly broke the silence as the tension mounted, because we hadn't a hope of surviving against four 109s, even if the pilots were inexperienced, which they probably weren't. Too many of them for comfort had fought in the Spanish Civil War. I was about to get Tubby Davies off the wireless set and send him down to Paton in the cabin to see if he knew what was happening when the intercomm clicked again. 'Gunner. The 109s have passed astern of us at about three miles range. Still on a southerly course!

'Fine! Paton, get the Lewis over to the port side, just in case they *do* have a go at us. Keep a good eye on them.'

Within a few seconds Paton came on.

'O.K. Dopey. Lewis on the port side. I can just about see the sods now, still going south. They can't have seen us.'

I ran on for five more minutes, during which the fighters and, eventually, the mountain tops of Norway, disappeared, throttled back to climbing revs and took her up to 2000 feet. Paton put the Lewis gun back in its stowage, replaced the two side windows and joined me in the cockpit.

'Look, as an exercise, would you like to get us back accurately on our homeward track?' I said to Paton. Now here are my notes, sorry about the writing.' I handed him my knee pad.

'We should have made departure from grid reference LKND 2607 at 1306, but I turned out to sea six minutes early and flew at 173 knots, not 140, on a course of 245 degrees magnetic for . . .' I glanced at my watch . . . ' seven minutes. I'll keep on this course for ten more minutes at 140 knots again. That should give you enough time to work out how to get back on our sweep at the correct time.'

Seven minutes later Paton came up from the nose with the chart and his figures.

'In three minutes alter course 42 degrees to port and, after seven minutes, circle for 3½ minutes before setting course for base on 240 degrees magnetic.' I checked. 'Looks good. Well done.'

In three minutes I turned on to 203 degrees and, as we neared the end of the seven-minute leg, called up Paton on the intercomm.

'Get a sea marker ready, Paton. One of the small ones will do as it's only got to last 3½ minutes. You can put it down the flare chute when I give the word.'

The sea marker was a container of extremely fine aluminium dust and the case disintegrated on hitting the sea, scattering the dust over an area of, perhaps, a twenty-yard circle, which gave a very visible mark. Depending on the roughness of the sea the particles could float for quite a considerable time. Had we not used the marker to circle we could, in that fresh wind, have been blown anything up to 2 miles downwind, a quite unacceptable error.

I came down to a hundred feet and said 'Half a minute to go, Paton.'

'Flare chute open,' came Paton's voice, 'Sea marker ready.'

'Drop,' I called and started to climb back to 2,000 feet, circling the aluminium mark. 3½ minutes later we set course on 245 degrees magnetic, back in the pattern of the sweep again.

'Would you like to take her home, Paton?' I asked.

We changed seats again.

'Keep a good lookout. The radio's been silent so nobody's found anything yet. But they might well have come up into our area from the South while we've been searching the fiords . . .'

Down in the nose again I ran a check on Paton's figures and confirmed that we'd rejoined the search pretty accurately, took a drift with the bombsight and went upstairs again.

'Wind's veering a little. Stick on one degree to starboard.'

'246 degrees it is, said Paton, twiddling the auto-pilot rudder control a fraction.

'Jolly good bit of navigation, that.' I said. 'We were lucky, of course, on two counts. One they didn't attack and two, because of that we've been able to sort out our navigation accurately. It's another matter altogether if you *are* attacked. Apart from the fact that you may be shot down, in which case navigation doesn't matter any more, or seriously damaged, there's one thing you can be sure of — your navigation will go to hell. You'll twist and turn during the attacks and could end up anything up to thirty miles away from estimate. And you'll use a lot of petrol, too. Bad things, 109s. Look, I'm sure you know this, anyway, but always turn *towards* whichever aircraft is attacking you at that particular time. I know that one's instinct is to turn away and try and get as far away from him as possible but it's a grave mistake. You'll present him with a much easier target, almost a non-deflection shot. Turn towards him and try to give him the worst shot in the book — crossing him at right angles. You need a slide rule to gauge that one and he'll waste an awful lot of his ammo on thin air.'

We continued our south-westerly track homewards until the intercomm came to life again.

'Hudson approaching,' called Paton.

I dashed up the stairs.

'Where?'

'Dead ahead.'

Four miles away the familiar outline was emerging from its background.

'Hold on a moment,' I said, 'There are three of them. There must be something up. Someone must have found something, that's a Battle Flight. Davies,' I called to the wireless operator, 'Have you had anything on the set?'

'Not a peep, sir. Nobody's reported anything on our frequency.'

'Some other squadron must have reported them then. Maybe 220 from Thornaby or 269 from Wick but, whoever they are, on this track they've come from Leuchars.'

I grabbed the Aldis signalling lamp.

'What's up?' I morsed to the leader.

[1]'*Hipper*, we think', came back the reply.

'Good luck' I just had time to get back to them before we flew right through the open formation of three 233 Squadron aircraft, waggling our wings in the usual greeting. In just over a minute they were invisible and, an hour later, Paton had landed us back at Leuchars.

Next day I filled in my log book . . .

"Hudson N7244 Self, P/O Paton, Cpl. Davies, LAC Morgan. Track Q, returning on Track R. Nothing seen." Just another routine patrol.

A few days later, at 0500, three crews assembled in the Ops. Room. They weren't very happy as the weather was rotten, the 'Haar' of the Scottish East Coast had settled in — the cloud was low, visibility bad and the raw sea mist bit into the one's bones. It was weather that we never flew in in peace-time and we were equally reluctant to do so now. Whatever else it was going to be it was going to be unpleasant and it had every promise of being lethal.

'It's the sort of weather that Mike Clarke copped it in a few months ago,' said Sergeant Muir to me. 'The same bloody haar.'

I agreed with him. I'd much rather have been in bed and I wished that Bill wasn't still on leave. Horan was to come as my second pilot. An Australian, he was another recent replacement for someone who'd been shot down last month and, however good he was, he wouldn't have the experience that was going to

[1]*Hipper* — a German cruiser.

be desirable on this trip. In the clag that we were going to have to fly through I would certainly be doing the flying myself and I was going to need some very smart navigating because it was well on the cards that we'd have to divert to another aerodrome at some stage of the proceedings.

Derry Matson was to fly the third aircraft.

'Derry, do me a favour, will you?' I asked.

'Certainly, Dopey, if I can. Anything to oblige.'

'Well look, if we both get diverted to Lossiemouth will you keep out of my hair and not do a bloody great swing into me like you did last time.'

'You're a fine one to talk. People who live in glass houses and so forth.'

'Now, gentlemen,' called the Controller, 'May I have your attention, please.' We're sorry to have to send you out in weather like this but it's just what the Hun's been looking for. We think he's running a convoy northwards to Trondheim. The navy are out after them and they want as much help from us as they can get as the visibility is so bad that each unit can't cover much sea. The more ships and aircraft the better but we feel they'll be hard to find. Two of you, Pilot Officer Matson and Sergeant Muir, will do four tracks of Patrol S.A.2., out on Tracks Q and S and back on Tracks R and T. Flying Officer Edwards will do Patrol L.8. Now it's likely that you may have to return early if the weather's too bad, or be delayed by trying to get round it. If so we want to know as soon as possible so I'll just remind you again of the procedure in such cases. Before you take off I want each navigator to hand to the Despatching Officer his Estimated Time of Return. If you have to come back early, work out just how many minutes earlier your new estimated time of return is and send the signal 'E' followed by that number of minutes. If you're going to be late then send 'L' followed by the corrected time. So 'E45' means that you're returning 45 minutes early and 'L73' means you're returning one hour and thirteen minutes late. Quite simple. On no account send your expected times of arrival; the enemy listens to all we say and can put two and two together. If you receive from us a diversion signal — again you have your codes for this — do not try to get back to base. It will mean that Leuchars has shut down from the weather point of view and you won't have an earthly of getting in. Go, as told, to your diversion aerodrome. Any questions?'

'Please may I join the Army, sir,' whispered L.A.C. Gilbert, my gunner, to me.

'No questions? Right. Good luck, all of you. Try and get airborne by 0700.'

We all went down to our crew room and got out the charts again, going over our navigation once more to check every detail. A few extra minutes on the ground could save precious seconds in the air.

'How long is your patrol?' I asked Sgt. Muir.

'Well, it's a straight out and straight back affair, with no frigging around the other end. We could be there and back in 4½ hours. Back for lunch, easily. Yours?'

'Well, we're a bit further north. Could do it in five and a half hours at least if we're lucky. But in this sort of weather I'd be happier with two hours petrol reserve for diversions. If we miss Fraserburgh to the north we've a hell of a long way to go up the Moray Firth before we hit land, and hit it is just what we're likely to do, we're right into the hills of Easter Ross there. I hope the target is worth it.'

By 0650 we were airborne into the *haar,* with ten-tenths cloud at 800 feet and the drizzle piling up opaquely on our wiperless windscreen. Forward I could see very little, sideways, as usual, was better but aircraft don't fly sideways; it's what's in front that counts. Like cliffs and hills.

'Departure point coming up in six minutes,' said Horan over the intercomm as we coast-crawled northwards, 'Steer 058 degrees magnetic from Stonehaven.'

'Horan, I'm taking her out to sea half a mile. Get a drift on this course, will you?'

'O.K.'

'Drift taken,' said Horan a minute later.

Good! He would have drawn a chinagraph pencil line on the compass bowl of the bombsight. When we turned out on our patrol line he would take another drift, draw another line and the intersection point would give us a fairly accurate wind speed and direction as a check on those of the met forecast. If they varied much a navigator with faith in his abilities would choose his own wind in such conditions. If Horan was doubtful he would probably ask my advice. At Stonehaven I turned on to 058 degrees magnetic.

'Steering 058 degrees magnetic, time of departure 0713,' I called down to Horan.

'When you've sorted things out down there you might as well come up here, there's a much better view and you might spot something you'd miss from down there.'

As Horan joined me I said 'Just keep popping down and taking a new drift every now and then; that's about all we can do'. The best view was sideways where, I suppose, we could see up to half a mile to a mile. Forward, things were distinguishable really at only about 400 yards or so, a distance we covered in five seconds. Subtract your reaction time and that didn't leave you much time to avoid an obstacle and the only quick avoiding action that the aircraft would respond to was a yank back on the control column, which would carry us straight up into the cloud. With the present cloud base we would be unable to descend through it again as it was getting lower and lower as we flew eastwards and we were being squeezed into an ever-decreasing amount of vertical airspace. Tension in the aircraft rose and a quietness descended on the speeding Hudson as we each sat in silent isolation. All four of us would be thinking one common thought — was there *any* point in carrying on this patrol? How much sea were we covering in our search — a band five hundred yards across? And in such dangerous conditions. We each had our own private worries, also. Just say we came upon the ships! Five seconds later they would be gone, lost astern of us. The best pilot in the world couldn't guarantee to hold a consistent Rate 2 turn in these conditions for exactly 360 degrees and hope to come upon the ships again, and I wasn't that pilot; I'd be more concerned with keeping my left wing tip from hitting the water. Horan had the responsibility for getting us back to land to make an accurate landfall on flat coastline, well away from cliffs and hills.

Tubby Davies and Gilly had no control over their fate at all. Uppermost in their minds would be the thought that it all depended on Horan to get us back to land and then on me to get the machine down on the deck safely. All they had was a pious hope that we'd pull it off, they knew that no guarantees were attached and that it wasn't going to be just skill that was going to get us out of this, there'd be a large element of luck as well.

Tubby came forward from his wireless set and handed Horan a message. Horan got weaving on the Syko deciphering machine and handed me the result . . .

'K 233 E220 repeat E220."

'That's Sgt. Muir's aircraft,' I said to Horan, 'He's packed it in already and returning to base three hours and forty minutes early.'

'Sensible fellow,' said Horan.

'Yes, it's not too good *here*. Look, I'm packing up this track. We'll go back and start again from a departure further north, but we can't go back on a reciprocal or we might hit those bloody cliffs; I just don't know this coastline well enough to be able to take you in to flat land. The only flat land I *know* is along the south coast of the Moray Firth between, say, Banff and Lossiemouth so we'll aim for that. I want you to get us up into the Moray Firth on a westerly heading at least twenty miles from that coast. When we're safely in we'll run south to the Portknockie area. I'm turning *now*, at 0752, on to 045 degrees magnetic. Draw a couple of lines on your chart, one north from Portnockie and, twenty miles up it, eastwards out into the drink. On this course we'll cut that line, so work it all out. No great hurry, I think it's going to take us about half an hour to get to that line so you'll have enough time to do your sums.'

I flew on in the murk, squeezed now to a couple of hundred feet off the leaden sea. The main cloud base was at about 300 feet but wisps drooped down from it and forced me lower. I *had* to keep lower; once I got into the cloud there was only one way to go — up. And just how we'd get down in the murk that seemed to cover the whole area I had no idea. Basically we couldn't. Once you got lost in that cloud you would have to take pot luck as to how you broke out of it. It there was any land at 300 feet or over then we were dead men if we came down. We could always bale out, of course, but most airmen had a primitive urge to stick with the aircraft for as long as possible, hoping that something would turn up, but not high ground.

Horan came out of the nose a quarter of an hour later.

'I've got it all sorted out, I think.' In eleven minutes we're turning in to the Moray Firth, course 282 degrees magnetic. Keep that for 22 minutes then on to 198 magnetic for Portknockie.'

'Well done. But the weather hasn't improved yet.' I took another glance at the altimeter. I'd come down to 185 feet. Things were getting marginally worse but, some time later, as we went Westward into the Moray Firth it improved a bit. We turned South for Portknockie and, as we neared the land, there was a definite improvement. We turned Eastwards.

'We'll set off again on a modified L8 from Peterhead. Lay off a track from there,' I told Horan.

Though the weather had improved it was relative. I could now fly at 300 feet, which took a deal of the strain off me, but the visibility was still poor, the cloud still ten-tenths and there was little apparent sign of this weather system clearing. We'd lost a lot of time in restarting and would have to watch our petrol. Quite soon after leaving Peterhead we were into the worsening weather again. As the minutes became an hour I found my altitude dropping to 250 feet, to 230, through the mental danger barrier of 200 down to 190 feet.

Tubby Davies came forward again and Horan decoded the message. "T 233 E150" it read. Derry Matson had now packed it in and was returning to Leuchars 2½ hours early. It confirmed my belief that there wasn't an earthly hope of the weather improving enough to give us the chance of getting through this front and doing an effective patrol the other side of it and that the sooner I got out of this stomach-churning flight the better. I got on the intercomm. 'O.K. chaps, we're packing it in.

'Horan, we'll do the same again. Northwest, then westward into the Moray Firth, but take us deeper in this time. We'll land at Lossiemouth so draw your north line through Lossie.'

As I turned northwest I cursed my lack of moral courage in not having the sense to turn back sooner and I thought back to our run in to Portknockie where the weather had been good enough for me to have slipped into Lossiemouth, because it was beginning to look as though I'd left my decision too late. Things were getting worse, not better. As though to hammer the lesson home Corporal Davies reappeared with a message.

'Decode it yourself, Tubby, Mr Horan's busy with the navigation.' A few minutes later he was handing me the decoded message.

'Hold it up in front of me, Tubby, I can't spare a hand.'

"Leuchars out Divert Thornaby" it read.

'THORNABY!' I cried, 'Bloody nonsense. I can't get to Thornaby from here; it must be all of 250 miles away.'

It could mean only one thing. They knew we were up in this area somewhere and it was their estimate that not only was Leuchars out but our obvious diversion aerodromes of Lossiemouth, Dyce and Montrose were out also. The considered opinion of experienced men assessing the situation in calm surroundings was that there was no way that I could get my aircraft safely to earth anywhere in Scotland.

We were on our own now. I *could* have got to Thornaby but the navigation errors after flying an additional 250 miles out of sight of land on top of our present dead-reckoning errors meant that we'd need a large reserve of fuel to find ourselves and get in and we hadn't got it. I knew Thornaby, having been stationed there in 1937, and I knew that any error to the south of track would take us into those damn great cliffs that ran down towards Whitby and Scarborough. I well recalled a trip before the war in weather far and away better than this with my navigator and me peering forward through our rain-obscured windscreen for the first sign of those great black cliffs that would smash us to fragments if we hit them. At the identical moment that my navigator shouted 'Cliffs' I had seen them too and put the wheel hard over to get the Anson into a vertical right-hand turn, then an equally steep left-hander as, once having found those menacing rocks, we didn't want to lose sight of them. Today the weather was far worse and I was flying a faster and heavier aircraft. In today's conditions I couldn't do what I did in that Anson, my nine-ton aircraft just wouldn't turn fast enough.

No, I was stuck with whatever lay up here in the north, Thornaby was out. We'd stick to my plan and make for Lossiemouth but, for the first time, the idea of climbing up through the clouds, flying half way into the Scottish mainland and then baling out was starting to form in my mind. But very much as a last resort, paramount was the primitive instinct to stay with the aircraft and get it, and us, safely to earth. It was instinct, and not reasoned thinking. A trained crew was a valuable asset, months, *years* of expensive training had been put into them and if the likelihood of the aircraft's crashing was above a certain percentage then it was pointless to throw away the crew as well, for nothing; let the aircraft crash and salvage the rest, the part that each of the four individuals on board knew was the most important. But say, after baling out to safety, the aircraft crashed into a town, or a school. What then? That would be something you'd have to live with for the rest of your life. O.K., with a war on it probably wasn't going to be all that long a life so you'd not suffer too much mental anguish of the sort one could visualise — 'Saw Dopey Edwards the other day. Remember him? Flew for seven hours in the shittiest weather we'd had for years and had to bale out over the Highlands. Damn nearly wore his shoes out walking eighteen miles to the first house. Pity about those schoolkids! Anyway, I'd stick with what we'd got for the moment. As we'd need all the fuel we'd got I leaned out the mixture, running the engines hotter than advisable, but it was going to give us a few more gallons and I might save a few more by getting Gilbert out of the turret so as to bring his weight forward and trim the aircraft better.

'Gilbert, you can't do any good back there. Come forward.' A minute later I was conscious that Gilly had joined us, standing behind the spar near Tubby Davies but I couldn't acknowledge him, I couldn't spare a fraction of a second's diversion from the concentration of keeping below every wisp of the cloud base and as far above the sea as possible. I just must not get into cloud or that wrecked schoolhouse would become a possibility. Horan came up from the nose after taking a drift. All four of us were now gathered together and I am sure that we felt happier that way, huddled in a close group to face the mutual danger together. Tubby Davies, like all wireless operators, sat and gazed at his set in suspended animation but the other two gazed steadily ahead with me, passing an occasional remark that got a short but understanding answer. I felt happier with them at my side as they seemed to bear me no resentment for the situation we were in and there was no doubt that, by the minute, things were getting worse. I would have thought, five minutes ago, that the leaden ball in my stomach was incapable of getting any heavier, that there *had* to be a limit to the amount of discomfort it could inflict on me. But it hadn't finished with me yet. As the sense of dread mounted so did the pain; it appeared to have limitless resources. And this, of course, was how Tinker Bell, Mike Clarke and Sgt. Hallam had died. I wondered how long the misery had lasted in their cases before the final, very swift ending. One should count one's blessings, of course; I'm sure that when it came, it would come so suddenly that there would be little additional terror, the realisation and the act would be almost simultaneous. But it was a hell of a way to go, really. One's mind raced on, one fantasised . . .

'Daddy, you know the heroes of the Great War.'

'What, chaps like Albert Ball and Rhys Davies?'

'Yes, that's right. A friend of mine says they all died gloriously, facing fearful odds. Is that right, Daddy?'

'Yes, son. That's quite correct.'

'Well, *you* died for your country too, Daddy, didn't you? Did *you* die facing fearful odds?'

'Yes, son. I certainly did.'

'Tell me about it, Daddy. Tell me *all* about it. Don't leave a thing out.'

'I hit a bloody hill, son.'

Horan had disappeared into the nose and now returned. 'Alter course to 282 degrees magnetic, Dopey. We're running into the Moray Firth.' I did a Rate One left turn, as much as I felt I could manage in my restricted airspace, and settled on our Westerly course, with no respite at all from the drear, drab *haar* and its accompanying stratus that grudged me every foot of altitude. Then, with a blow to my aching stomach, the fates put the boot in

21 July 1940. I led four aircraft to attack this blockade-running supply ship, the 'Normark', sister ship of the prison ship, 'Altmark'. While we probably hit her with two two-fifty pounders two of our aircraft were shot down, the 50 per cent casualty rate being rather a high price to pay. But shipping strikes were usually rather hairy affairs. The shadow of one of the attacking Hudsons can be seen at the stern of the ship. (I.W.M.)

My logbook entry for the night bombing trip to Hamburg on 18 April 1940.

YEAR 1940 MONTH	DATE	AIRCRAFT Type	No.	PILOT, OR 1ST PILOT	2ND PILOT, PUPIL OR PASSENGER	DUTY (INCLUDING RESULTS AND REMARKS)
MAY Time of Take-off		—	—	—	—	— TOTALS BROUGHT FORWARD
0815	13th	HUDSON	N7340	SELF	P/O Tacon L.A.C. Todd P/O Holland	Patrol L8
0725	15th	"	"	"	P/O Tacon Cpl. Davies P/O Holland	Recco of Norwegian Coast. Abandoned due to weather.
0640	17th	"	N7254	"	—"—	Search for a German convoy in the Skagerrak. Not found.
1115	18th	"	N7340	"	P/O Tacon L.A.C. Campbell P/O Holland	Leuchars – North Coates Fitties
2125	18th	"	"	"	—"—	Up the Elbe to Hamburg at nought feet. My Gawd! Another bloody burst tyre Campbell slightly wounded.
1120	20th	"	"	"	—"—	North Coates – Leuchars Nearly slain by Tacon on St. Andrews beach.
~~1040~~	22nd	"	"			
1040	22nd	"	"	"	F/O Davies 4 Crew	Leuchars – Silloth
1530	22nd	"	"	"	"	Silloth – Leuchars
1725	28th	"	"	"	P/O Paton Cpl. Davies L.A.C. Morgan	Track Q returning on Track R. Nothing seen.

GRAND TOTAL [Cols. (1) to (10)]
1144 Hrs. 05 Mins.

TOTALS CARRIED FORWARD

Bill Tacon's near-accident on the way home.

233 Squadron's Operational Record Book entry for the Hamburg raid.

Unable to drop bombs due to being blinded by searchlights for half an hour. Picked up by 5 searchlights at Cuxhaven. Dived to 200 feet and proceeded up the River Elbe. At Brunsbuttel very heavy A.A. fire in front of a/c and 11 search-lights. Further fire and lights at Gluksted. Forced to keep low in banks of river and could not drop bombs so returned and on the way dropped 4x250 lb. G.P. bombs on an aerodrome 2 milessouth of Stade, but only one exploded due to damaged electrical circuits due to hits from A.A. fire encountered earlier. Wireless unservica able from hits.

Year 1940 Month	Date	AIRCRAFT Type	No.	Pilot, or 1st Pilot	2nd Pilot, Pupil or Passenger	DUTY (Including Results and Remarks)
APRIL time of take-off	—	—	—	—	—	— Totals Brought Forward
115	17	Hudson	N7254	SELF	P/O Tacon Cpl. Purves L.A.C. McAdie Lt. Cdr. Fleming T.A.S., R.N.	Nine 25lb. Incendiaries on Stavanger 'Drome. Spotting for H.M.S. "Suffolk". Attacked by Ju88. Gunner drove him off damaged. Five hits on us.
515	19	"	N7224	"	P/O Tacon Cpl. Purves L.A.C. Gilbert	Track E. Recco of Björne Fiord and Haugesund. Hits by ground machine gun in starboard engine. Tried to fly under a bridge. Didn't. Home on one engine.
910	20	"	N7224	"	P/O Tacon Cpl. Purves L.A.C. Gilbert.	Night recco of Frederikshavn (Danmark) for "Admiral von Scheer". Not there. Fired on by solitary pom-pom. No hits on us.
630	24	"	N7240	"	P/O Tacon L.A.C. Davies Cpl. Burnett	Protection of 3 Destroyers. Jumped by 2 Me109's. Landed Lossiemouth. Swung on landing & nearly hit Derry Matson. My port tyre burst & Derry's starboard
115	25	"	N7240	"	"	Lossiemouth - Leuchars.
0930	29	"	N7246	"	F/Sgt. Axe L.A.C. Walton L.A.C. Walker	Track J. Landed at Lossiemouth on W/T orders. Dicey weather
						TOTAL FLYING APRIL

GRAND TOTAL [Cols. (1) to (10)] 1074 Hrs. 40 Mins. — Totals Carried Forward

A busy week.

Officers and NCO's of No. 233 Squadron in March 1939, Anson in background. Author front row, 4th from right. Other characters mentioned in the book – centre the CO, Wing Commander Lewis George le Blount Croke, 'Louis'. Hudson crash on second day of the war – the two killed were Guy Robinson, front row, 2nd from right, and Godfrey, front, 6th from left. Sgt Hallam, my rude second pilot in my crash into the river Eden 18 October 1939, 2nd row, 4th from right. Killed in a crash a few weeks later. Wallis, killed with Squadron Leader Feeney, our second-in-command, attacking the 'Scharnhost', front row, extreme right.

1982. Author in the cockpit of a Spitfire, 41 years after he first flew one. (Mike and Pam Parker)

further as it hit me forcibly that I had seriously miscalculated our fuel reserves. At an adequate altitude we could run each of our four petrol tanks dry if we were really going for endurance. As the tank emptied the engines spluttered and cut irregularly, one before the other, and the aircraft lost a bit of height. I couldn't risk anything of that nature, I'd have to leave about ten gallons in each tank, and that was going to be thirty gallons of unusable petrol, a very big loss indeed and a half-hour inroad into our safety margin.

I went through my options:-

1. With luck we'd get into Lossiemouth. It was right on the coast and there were only a few sand dunes to clear.
2. Montrose would be my second choice. Very similiar situation to Lossie's
3. Dyce I was least happy about, I didn't know it all that well.
4. Undoubtedly the bit of coastline I knew best was that from Leuchars north to Montrose, all of it flat as long as you didn't go more than a mile inland, with the beach to the North of St. Andrews as a small additional bonus. I could keep it as a last resort and if that failed we *could,* of course, bale out. If we flew just a few miles inland I could let the other three bale out, turn the aircraft round and point it out to sea with the auto-pilot engaged before I took to my brolly, too.
5. I could land on a beach, probably wheels-up in a belly flop in case the sand was soft and turned us over.

On we flew into the unending murk. Horan appeared. 'Alter course left to 188 degrees magnetic. We're running into Lossiemouth now. ETA about five minutes, but it could be anything up to three minutes either side.' So from now on we had to keep our eyes peeled. And the cloud base was getting even lower. Even at 100 feet I still sped through the occasional wisp of cloud 'I don't think I can make this,' I shouted to Horan. 'Those sand dunes are going to shove me up into the cloud. We've still got petrol. As soon as I see the coast I'm turning East.'

But I knew as I said it that there was little hope of reaching Montrose. We'd been flying for 6½ hours already and Montrose would have been all of 150 miles away along the coast, Eastwards to Fraserburgh then Southwards past Peterhead and Aberdeen. Were we *really* going to have to bale out? But however unintelligent or obtuse my reasoning, that was going to be my last resort. I considered the beaches as they sped past below the nose — this one too rough a surface, that too much cut up with little burns running across it to the sea, on *this* one the tide mark came right up to the dunes — the Hudson would become awash at high tide. There was nothing there that I'd really like to stick the aircraft down on but, if that's all that was going to turn up I might as well do it soon. My mind was made up for me, however. We ran out of beaches and into rocky foreshore, mile after mile of it. And cliffs. But, as we ran south near Peterhead there was a definite improvement. Even through the obscurity of the water-streaked windscreen I could see about half a mile ahead and I was up at a comparitively luxurious 250 feet.

'If this carries on I'll have a crack at Dyce,' I called to Horan. 'I know roughly where it is.' As Aberdeen harbour came in view I turned sharply right and roared over the city north-westerly at 200 feet, lowering my undercarriage as I did so; I wanted everything ready for a snap landing — mixtures full rich, airscrews fully fine, petrol selector to my fullest tank 'I'm following the road and as soon as the boundary comes up I'm going in.' I said to Horan.

'The wind's Easterly,' said Horan helpfully.

'Not much of it though. I'll land downwind. Keep a good lookout to port and shout if you see the aerodrome before I do.' As we flew up the road I throttled back to 110 knots and put down 30 per cent of flap. At the same time Horan and I saw the grass of the aerodrome. I knocked the flap lever down and left it there, in that position it would put on full flap for me and hold it. I gave the engines a burst of throttle to cover my steep turn in to the field, wound the tail trim hard back and hoped that I was pointing in a good direction, as we couldn't see the far boundary of the aerodrome in the mist. I'd guessed O.K. and we rumbled to a stop, seven hours to the minute after we'd taken off from Leuchars, It had been a very long seven hours indeed.

I took my time about taxying in, pulling in the flaps and opening the engine cooling gills before making a leisurely progress towards the hangars and the deserted apron. I switched off the engines and we all got out and stretched. We said little, because there's not an awful lot you *can* say after you've been under a pall of tension with nothing positive, nothing useful to show for your efforts. As airmen you don't really make an awful lot of fuss about the fact that you're glad to be on Mother Earth again. But damned glad we were, without a shadow of doubt.

When we got home again to Leuchars the next day we reported into the Ops Room where the Intelligence Officer de-briefed us. His report read:- "Patrol L8. A/c[1] encountered very bad weather making it impossible to carry out patrol. A/c proceeded to

[1] A/c — Aircraft.

Peterhead, where course was set to carry out a similiar patrol to L8. At 1150 A/c received a signal to land at Thornaby, but as petrol was running short it was decided to land at Lossiemouth, but low cloud prevented this and A/c eventually landed at Dyce. Nothing to report during the entire trip."

As one's flying log book doesn't have enough space for the story of one's life my own entry was a bit shorter:- "L8. Landed Dyce."

It was all a bit maddening. Nothing heroic to show for our efforts, no ships sighted or sunk, not a thing that would help the war effort. Pity it had all been so bloody dangerous!

I did the next trip with another new boy whose father was a well-known comedian. The briefing had been odd as it placed some sort of embargo on attacking merchant shipping, and this was the second time that such a restriction had been placed upon me. About three weeks before, after flying with Bill on a met flight, I had entered in my log book the negative statement 'Weather report of Norwegian Coast. Machine-gunned by troopship. No hits on us.' While a low level attack on a ship whose decks were crammed with rifle-toting soldiers could have been hairy, as they could have got off the better part of two hundred bullets in each volley in addition to the normal machine-gun and light automatic fire from the ship's crew, it seemed at the time quite extraordinary to leave unscathed a shipload that was going to give our overstretched Army an even worse time but, like good boys, we brought our bombs home because our lords and masters obviously had their motives; they knew best. I was almost *sure* they did.

Similarly on this flight. 'You are to attack a merchant ship only if it attacks you,' had said the Controller, or something like it. I pointed out that I've never had a 4,000-ton merchant ship take off from the sea and do a quarter attack on me.

'You know perfectly well what I mean, Dopey, don't live up to your name. Alright, I'll re-word that. If you approach a ship and it opens fire at you then you can reply. Otherwise leave it alone. Now, your task today is a reconnaissance of Bergen harbour. It's stuffed full of merchant shipping, the vast majority Norwegian impressed into German service. Now don't start blowing Norwegians to Kingdom Come, for God's sake.

With Roy navigating we ran low into the Norwegian coast, about a hundred feet off the deck, to evade their radar and went up to a couple of thousand feet for the recce.

'My God', said Roy, 'How the hell can I cope with that lot.

There must be fifty ships in the place. I'd need a stenographer to get this down accurately.'

'Get her to make a note of these shell bursts too, while she's at it, would you,' I said, 'Now get a move on before someone hits us.'

Apart from the light automatic flak that was coming up at us there was a scattering of heavy anti-aircraft shell bursts. One of their batteries must be a fair distance away and firing with very flat trajectories as an 88 m.m. flak gun couldn't normally traverse fast enough on a low-flying target. But the really worrying stuff was the endless light automatic fire that reached its lethal smoke trails up at us like clutching fingers.

'I've made as good a job as I can,' Roy said after a while, 'Just numbers by approximate tonnage. But you know that there are two of those ships firing at us don't you? They must be German-manned.'

'O.K. We'll give them the two-fifties then, a couple apiece. That'll teach 'em.' 'Not on, old boy. They're both moored in the middle of groups of ships. You could never pick them out.'

I took a look down. From the centre ship of a group of five moored abreast of each other rose a stream of tracer gunfire and I realised that Roy was right, there wasn't a hope of planting my bombs without hitting the other ships. I felt enraged at the ease with which he could fire at me with apparent immunity.

'Hang on, Roy we'll have one quick crack at him.' I rammed the nose down into a diving turn, the speed building up so rapidly that I throttled right back to give me more time at him, and thumbed the gun button. The two guns on the ship and I swopped gunfire as the range closed, I could see my tracers and incendiaries ricocheting all over his decks but both guns kept firing back. A shot went through the wing. Another. I was running out of airspace and could fire no more, a disadvantage not shared by the Germans. As I stopped firing I hauled back on the stick with all my might and just missed his masthead as one more shot went through the fuselage. 'Where's the second one!' I asked Roy when we'd regained height.

'That black one with white upperworks, third in of that group. But just look at all this shit they're loosing off at us!'

He was quite right, of course. The intensity of the flak was considerable and I wasn't going to do any real damage to a ship with machine-gun fire.

'O.K. Let's get the hell out of it.'

At about 500 feet we fled southwards out of the port, rose over the hills and, as we slid down the other side, a group of oil storage tanks appeared. They'd do! There was no time for Roy to get to work, I'd drop the bombs myself. I snapped the bomb door lever to 'Open' and yelled to him 'Are the bombs fused 'Live' and is the Mickey Mouse[1] set.'

'Yes to both' he shouted back.

The 'Bomb Doors Open' light flashed on the dashboard, I climbed up a bit, a couple of hundred feet, to ensure that the bombs had enough height to arm themselves and, when I judged the time to be right, jabbed my thumb on the bomb release button on the control wheel. As I put the bomb door lever to 'Closed' I turned to watch the explosions of our four-second delayed bombs. The gouts of earth rose up, one fairly close, but not, alas, close enough to blow up the tank and we sailed upwards to fly into the peaceful country to the north of Bjornefiord.

As we flew southwards a ship of about 2,000 tons was sailing towards us. Maddeningly, now that we'd dropped our bombs, it flew the Nazi flag. The crew appeared not to have noticed us as no gunfire was loosed off in our direction so I circled round, climbed so as to give myself a longer dive, and shoved the nose down, attacking from the bow. I put the gunsight on the bridge and thumbed the gun button in the longest burst of my life. The Brownings in the nose hammered out their forty shots a second, cordite fumes filled the cockpit, I could see my bullet hits winking away on the steelwork of the bridge then suddenly, there was an explosion up in the nose. Something had hit us there and, if they'd hit us once they could do it again. I sailed on southwards towards the open sea and sent Roy down into the nose to assess the damage. He returned after a while complaining of the fact that he couldn't see across the navigator's compartment for gunsmoke and, anyway, he couldn't see any damage at all.

'Then what the hell was that big bang?' I said. 'And the pressure wave?'

'Search me!'

'You really can't see anything wrong?!

'No. Not a thing.'

'O.K. We'll go home now. Give me a course from the exit from Bjornefiord.'

As we left I saw on the water, quite close together, three floating mines. They looked like British ones and would have broken away during a recent storm from a minefield laid by us. My initial reaction was to leave them as although, by international law, mines are supposed to render themselves safe when they snap their moorings it doesn't always happen, in which case these could still clobber an enemy ship at night for example. But our Navy also operated in these waters, of course, and we wouldn't want them to be hoist with their own petards. I decided to try and sink them, and one does this with a certain amount of circumspection. The idea is, hopefully, to hit the casing with armour-piercing bullets so that the mine slowly sinks, and to hope that one of the horns isn't hit and detonated. A mine going off on the surface raises a huge waterspout that could seriously damage any aircraft flying through it, as well as sending dozens of fragments of its metal casing through the air, each one of which could be lethal. So you don't want to get too near it in your dive, but it's such a small target that it's difficult to hit without getting close so the success rate is, as you may imagine, low. Very low in my case as I'd no sooner opened fire than it became apparent that only my left gun was working and this stopped firing after a second or so, out of ammunition. It was the first time I'd found myself over hostile territory and out of ammunition, and it gave me a great feeling of insecurity. I turned on the taps and fled out to sea.

After we landed we could still find no entry hole for whatever exploded up in the nose and the mystery remained unsolved until the armourer came to clean and reload my front guns. The right-hand gun had jammed with (only) thirteen rounds left in the ammunition tank and the jam was caused by a round in the feedway which had exploded. I had fired such a long burst at the ship that the guns had got exceedingly hot, the right one so much so that the round in the feedway, in the twentieth of a second that it remained there before it was due to be rammed into the breech, had cooked off. The gun must have been nearly white hot.

'We'll put new barrels into these guns, Sir,' the armourer said. They won't be an awful lot of use after this.'

[1]Mickey Mouse — automatic bomb-release mechanism for spacing bombs to a pre-set interval.

Chapter 7

The battle in France was going badly, Holland already having been over-run, and, ten days after our night trip to Hamburg, Belgium had surrendered leaving the British and French armies in an impossible position, the British Army being forced back on Dunkirk. The Coastal Command squadrons further south were involved in the evacuation of Dunkirk but we were still fully occupied with the Norwegian campaign and it was to be another fortnight before the British Army was finally evacuated, on 10 June, the day that Mussolini decided that it was time he brought Italy into the war on Hitler's side for some easy pickings. Two days earlier yet another aircraft carrier, the *Glorious,* had been sunk off Norway.

It must have been about this time that I found myself in command of B Flight. Cooper, our Flight Commander, and Dai Davies had gone off with their Hudson on some mysterious detachment from which they never returned to the squadron. Later we heard rumours that they had ended up in North Africa and eventually that they had been shot down and taken prisoners. Whether or not the rumours were correct I don't know, but I sent a couple of quid off to a fund which was organised to send out books and games to prisoners of war, as I could imagine nothing worse for an airman, used to the freedom of the skies, than the boredom of being cooped up in a prison camp, and asked if they could get some stuff to Coope and Dai. I don't suppose they ever got it and they must have been liberated eventually as I heard that Cooper had been killed later, though where I don't know. Anyway, as the senior surviving officer in B Flight, I inherited the Flight but not, unfortunately, the acting rank and pay of a Flight Lieutenant, as Cooper was still officially a member of the squadron, and I stooged out the rest of my time as a Flying Officer; all very frustrating.

The anti-aircraft defences of the Norwegian ports now seemed to be increasing. With all ground fighting a thing of the past, the Hun could concentrate his resources on fixed targets likely to be visited by the RAF, chiefly the ports and aerodromes. On a trip to Kristiansand in the Skagerrak, when I was navigating, I remember watching some of the flak coming up at us as I concentrated on the bombsight, the 40 mm tracer throwing out the smoke in spirals but it didn't seem anything to worry about unduly. We kept the vertical camera running doing line overlaps across the harbour as we ran in to the aerodrome to drop our bombs on the runway and I was surprised when Bill, after getting my 'Bombs gone' call over the intercom, did a rapid turn away making it difficult to observe our bomb bursts. We were supposed to go on and do a recce of Stavanger afterwards, but we'd had difficulty in finding Kristiansand in heavy rain and low cloud in the Skagerrak and hadn't the petrol to get up to Stavanger, so we came straight home. In the Ops Room I was giving my report on the recce to the Intelligence Officer and happened to mention the slight flak to which we were subjected when Bill Tacon and Bill Paice, the gunner, simultaneously exploded into the 1940 equivalent of 'You must be joking!' They were so adamant about it that I conceded defeat. Apparently a lot of stuff had been flung at us but it must have been chiefly above the level of my vision, looking downwards through the transparent bombing panel. I was too busy with my bombsight to study it in detail whereas the two Bills up on the top deck had had a grandstand view.

There was a pronounced difference of attitude between the pilot and the navigator during a high-level bombing run, all the more remarkable because we both did both jobs, turn and turn about, despite which one forgot the other's viewpoint. The bomb-aimer was extremely busy. Having put into the bombsight the settings for airspeed, height, barometric pressure, bomb terminal velocity and trail angle, wind speed and direction and enemy speed and direction if you were bombing ships, he then had to guide the pilot towards the target with steering instructions. It was solid concentration, watching the target move down the drift wires and trying to correct the inevitable pilot errors in speed and height-keeping by altering the input to the sight and its levelling screws. Your concentration much reduced the natural feeling of apprehension of an intruder over enemy territory and a long way from home. If the pilot was twitchy that was *his* affair.

The pilot, on the other hand, despite his having to concentrate on the accuracy of his flying, saw more of the danger and had to watch out for anything new. His job not being so mentally active, he had more time to get worried so that his conversational style tended to be of the 'How much bloody longer?' type as opposed to the more soothing, cooing approach of the bomb-aimer who, while getting across his regret that the pilot's training appeared to have been carried out principally on the Big Dipper at Blackpool, he was not to worry, but just to carry out the eminently sensible instructions he was receiving . . . 'Right a bit . . . riiiight . . . Steady . . . Steady at that . . . Left-left . . . Steady . . . Steaaady . . . Fine. What's that you said? No, the bombs haven't hit. How can they? I haven't even dropped them yet . . . Oh! *Tit.* No, I haven't pressed the tit yet. Any minute now. . . . Left-left a fraction . . . Steady at that . . . Right a touch . . . Steady, steady. Bombs gone.'

As you gave the 'Bombs gone' the yellow, fish-like shapes of the bombs appeared in your vision as they fell away, the nose vanes a whirring blur if the bombs were nose-fused. With a few minnow-like wriggles as they adjusted themselves to the slipstream they slid rapidly downwards and diminshed in size as they took up a nose-down attitude as their vertical speed increased. Eventually they became merely tiny dots moving along with, but slightly behind, you until they vanished completely, the smoke of the first burst on the ground being followed rapidly by the others, marching ahead of it. One only had the leisure to watch them on an undefended target, the normal pattern being that, as soon as you called 'Bombs gone' the engines went to full throttle and the aircraft went into a steep turn into the quickest, or safest, getaway direction. I often pondered on our habit of going in on high level bombing at cruising speed. It wouldn't have used much extra petrol just to go at full throttle for five minutes while approaching the target, and one would have been in the danger area for a shorter time, but I can never remember doing this. Like trained mice we sailed in at our standard 140 knots indicated and at 'Bombs gone' the pilot heaved up the bomb-door lever, shoved the throttles to the gate and turned smartly homewards. Pavlov's dogs couldn't have done better. But, however much I pondered, I at least never changed my system, though maybe there were more intelligent types in the squadron. I never enquired.

A couple of days after, my attention was drawn to the increasing amount of flak (the squadron Operations Book notes it to be 'heavy') at Bergen when we led Piejus and Troughten-Smith's Hudson on a bombing run on the harbour, and Piejus's Hudson collected a few hits. We were undamaged. I suppose they were aiming at me and consequently hitting the second aircraft, which is as it should be. All-in-all, however, it was becoming obvious that the Hun was getting better organised on the ground and we had a busy time trying to plot new gun positions; not that we could do this all that accurately, an incentive to leave the area being provided by the gun you might be trying to plot going into action. As we left Bergen below the level of the hills to the seaward side of the harbour I had my window open and heard a machine-gun firing *down* on us from further up the hill. We gave him best, and continued on home. After that chap at Haugesund had plugged up one engine for me a few weeks earlier, I had lost interest in trying to damage a hundred-pound's worth of machine gun by putting a whole aircraft and crew at risk in order to do it.

During the next few days something important was thought to be at sea and we, and 224 Squadron, did quite a few additional patrols along the coast. On 21 June I patrolled an eighty-mile stretch from Bergen down to Karmo without seeing anything except a rapidly diving submarine in a restricted bombing area, but, 100 miles to the north, Derry Matson and Badoux, working southwards from Bermanger, were having an eventful time. After making an abortive attack on a merchant ship, which failed because an electrical fault caused the bombs to drop off the racks the moment the bomb doors opened, they were chased into cloud by a couple of fighters. They hid in this for a while and on emerging at 1,500 feet they sighted the 26,000 ton battle cruiser *Scharnhorst* with an escort of half a dozen destroyers. An urgent signal was sent to base and all aircraft within range were ordered to attack her. By this time we were well on our way home and had insufficient petrol to get anywhere near her and I ought to be ashamed of the fact that a feeling of relief swept over me as we checked the *Scharnhorst's* position and found we couldn't get to her. She was 26,000 tons of hell on earth. Apart from her main armament of nine 11-inch guns and twelve 5.9s she carried fourteen 4.1-inch anti-aircraft guns, sixteen 37 mm and an assortment of machine-guns. Worse, far worse, would be her umbrella of fighters — 109s and 110s. The war had been going on too long for our particular brand of heroism to last. We flew thankfully homewards and spared a thought for those less fortunate. We had been carrying four two-fifty pound GP bombs in case we had met shipping but they'd have been absolutely useless against the *Scharnhost;* they wouldn't get through her armoured decks and would only blow a few deck fittings off her. It would have been a pretty useless gesture to risk your bacon for.

Anyway, it was an academic mental exercise as we couldn't get there. Soon after we landed a hurriedly assembled striking force of eight aircraft from 233 and 224 squadrons got away loaded with two 500 lb semi armour-piercing bombs apiece. Those aircraft that found the *Scharnhorst* were met by an overwhelming fighter cover of between 30 and 40 Messerschmitt 109s and 110s. Our second-in-command, Squadron Leader Feeney, with Andy Wallis, was shot down in flames; other aircraft were badly mauled in the attack, after which they landed at Sumburgh Head, in the Shetlands, as their nearest refuelling point. When last seen the *Scharnhorst* was going north-eastwards on a track of about 065 degrees true and, if she kept this up, would be well away from our patrol area by the morning.

The Royal Navy was still out in force, however, hunting for her and her supporting ships, so they needed air cover. Early the next day I led a flight of three aircraft on one such sortie, and it's an indication of the relative strengths of the Luftwaffe and the RAF, and of the distances which each had to fly to their operating areas, that whereas the Hun had continuously put 30 to 40 fighters over the *Scharnhorst* as she slipped up their coastline, it was quite an effort for us to dig out the odd flight of three aircraft over and above the normal patrolling duties of the squadron. And those aircraft were slow, heavy, under-armed and capable of remaining with their charges only for an hour or two.

We got away from Leuchars at 0545 hours. I had Immelman and Over of A Flight as Nos. 2 and 3 and, by 0708 hours, we'd come up with a couple of our cruisers which we escorted until 0735 hours, when we left them to go to a second force of four cruisers and a destroyer which was being shadowed by a Dornier 18K flying boat. The Dornier 18K was a twin-engined machine in which the engines were mounted in tandem in the mid-line, one puller and one pusher (see the photograph). It was armed with two Rheinmetal machine-guns mounted one in each of the open gun cockpits on a gun ring. One cockpit was in the bow and the other amidships. Belting away, not very far from the gunners, were the two airscrews. The field of fire of the front gunner was limited to the rear by the front airscrew just behind him and that of the midships gunner by the tail unit to the rear, and forwards by the rear airscrew. I attacked immediately with my fixed front guns and Bill stood alongside me as I fired, giving his opinion as to any corrections needed in my shooting which it appeared, were many. It wasn't that Bill was all that rude, really, it's just that it's quite difficult to hit a moving aircraft.

The Dornier climbed for the cloud layer above and, by the time we got to work on him, he was getting fairly near safety. I got off a few long bursts but Bill said that a lot of the stuff was going underneath him. I gave a long squirt, took my face from the gunsight, and watched the tracer, which seemed to confirm Bill's opinion; I was under-estimating his rate of climb. I raised the sight a bit and gave him a final long burst but he disappeared into the safety of the clouds. This was a great disappointment as, no doubt, he would wait around for a while and then return to continue shadowing our ships. It was a constant anxiety escorting convoys in this area because, apart from U-boats, we were so close to the Norwegian coastline that the Luftwaffe had little difficulty in putting bombers into the air from Stavanger and Kristiansand. Our convoys had a far safer journey if we could keep all shadowing aircraft away. As this was normally impossible we aimed at least at keeping them so far from the convoy that their reporting of the course and speed of the ships would be as inaccurate as possible. On the off chance that the Dornier might climb straight through the cloud and break cover on top, so giving us another shot at him, I followed him into the cloud.

It seemed to be a pretty thick layer of cloud so I throttled back to climbing revs and decided to put in the automatic pilot, an excellent Sperry that took a lot of hard work off our hands. I had lined up the three indices — rudder, aileron and elevator — and was about to click the pilot into engagement when something made me look through the windscreen ahead. I had a real fright to see, black and enormous and tremendously forbidding, the 18K in the cloud about 30 yards ahead. It looked very sinister, not only because the mist and fog of the cloud softened the outlines and made the whole scene look largely black in colour but because the waist gunner saw me at about the same time as I saw him. In his open cockpit, and clad in his black leathers and goggles, he looked like an executioner as he went for his gun. For my part there was no time for the niceties of sighting, I was a little higher than the Dornier, a bit off to the left, and we were overhauling him. I put my thumb on the gun button, rammed the nose down and swung right to hosepipe the stuff into the target. The clattering of the Brownings and the renewed smell of cordite fumes were of some comfort and I could see my tracer and incendiary bouncing off his push-pull engines, but the overpowering black figure crouched over his machine gun was all I could think about as I tried to hold my aim somewhere on the vital cockpit-engine area of the Dornier. To my intense relief I saw him slide out of sight and his gun cocked up in the air as he was hit. I remember sparing him the thought 'Poor devil', but it was all the time I could give him as, at that moment, our right wing got into the 18K's slipstream and we swung in astern of him, wallowing all over the place. I was intensely conscious of minute details of the enemy, of the hundreds of rivets in his metal skin, the hinges of his rudder, the wind-deflector in front of the gunner's cockpit, of the old-fashioned type of gun mounting with the Rheinmetal MG15 cocked drunkenly on it, of wireless loops and aerials, radiator outlets and a hundred and one things that I took in in the split second before, I thought, we were going to collide.

There was no further hope of hitting him with gunfire as we wallowed in his wake so I stopped firing and tried to regain control of the bucketing pig of a Hudson, with its semi-stalled right wing, before I carved his rudder to fragments with our starboard propeller. Eventually the wing pulled out of the suction and we slid over to the left, still overtaking. With no hope of slowing down in time we were now coming into the view of his front gunner, a repeat of the black menace in the waist cockpit, who waited for us to slide from behind the protection of his front airscrew, which was blanketing his field of fire to the rear. Those who have an interest in portrait painting will appreciate the expression 'head and shoulders three-quarters sinister, gaze directed at spectator.' Believe me, this gunner was 100 per cent sinister, none of your effete 75 per cent stuff, and his gaze was certainly directed at spectator, albeit along the barrel of his Rheinmetal. With a desperate feeling of complete helplessness because my guns would no longer bear, I derived some comfort from the fact that I thought I felt the Hudson yaw in towards the Dornier, as it would have done if our gunner was at that moment swinging his turret forward to join in the action, but I knew that we would slide into the Dornier gunner's field of fire before our gunner could get a shot clear of our own starboard airscrew, even if he could train his turret forward in time. The pre-battle prayer of the crew of Captain Horatio Hornblower, R.N., flitted through my mind. 'For what we are about to receive may the Lord make us truly thankful.'

It's a reflection upon how self-centred one tends to get that all I could think of was that I was scared rigid, and couldn't prevent myself from ducking my head below window level to shut out the sight of that dreadful black devil and his gun. It wasn't the slightest good doing it, of course; a bullet would come through the metal skin of the aircraft as easily as it would through the glass of the window, but I just couldn't face him. His position must have been equally awful really. Tucked up in his cloud and relaxing, no doubt, he would suddenly hear, and then see, our bullets crackling around his head and off the engines and also be aware that the return fire from his crewmate in the rear cockpit had ceased, for obvious reasons. He had to wait those agonising seconds during which he could see us through the airscrew disc but be unable to fire until we cleared it, and be well aware of our dorsal turret swinging forward to wreak its havoc on him with its twin Brownings.

In the end, however, he won. Our turret didn't make it in time. As I ducked, then raised my head yet again like a hypnotised rabbit, we slid from the protection of his airscrew and the muzzle of the Rheinmetal, down which I looked from 20 yards away, flashed red as he opened fire. A bullet going through a Hudson, or any other metal aircraft for that matter, makes a noise rather like cracking a whip and smashing a glass window at the same time. At twenty shots a second the burst that hit us seemed to make about a hundred times the noise. The shattering, splintering, crashing noise that seemed to start just above my head receded only slightly in volume as a line of bullets started about six inches above me and swept backwards through the top of the wireless set and into the cabin. It sounded as though the aircraft was being destroyed about our ears. But the gunner shot about a foot too high and stopped a yard too soon. That much lower and longer and he would have killed both pilots and the gunner, and probably the wireless operator as well. By this time I'd had a bellyful and had the wheel hard over, and the big, black shape of the Dornier and its winking front gun receded into the mist, vanished, and the noise and destruction ceased.

I ended up in a steep diving turn in the cloud, sorted it out and then we dropped down rapidly to see if the Dornier would fall out of the cloud as I was sure that I had at least done his engines a lot of no good. However, he didn't reappear in the next few minutes, which was a great disappointment because if he was still in flying trim he'd be reporting on our ships again. So I returned to our cruisers, to find Over still with them but not Immelman. Apparently he had lost us after the first attack on the Dornier and had found some other ships to escort, which would have pleased them, no doubt. Over and I continued our escort until the limit of our fuel and Immelman landed back at Leuchars about 20 minutes after we did.

Most air action is rather impersonal, except within the confines of your own crew and aircraft, but the bar room brawl type of shoot-out with the Dornier in the cloud was on quite a different, and highly personal plane. I'll never forget those menacing, black-clad gunners, and I still feel sorry for the one in the waist cockpit. I suppose we shot him but it would be nice, now, to think that maybe he'd finished a banana before we arrived on the scene and had just slipped on the skin, or something.

In the Ops Room they told us that France had now finally surrendered. Although I was politically and historically unconscious in those days I remember feeling, despite the apparently hopeless position we were in — imprisoned in our island with completely inadequate arms — a distinct feeling of relief that, at last, we could run the show on our own. The whole war seemed simpler now and it never occurred to me that logically we would probably lose it. What saved us, of course, was the English Channel. If we'd been part of the mainland of Europe we would have followed the rest of the continent into bondage. With the unforgettable and inspiring leadership of Winston Churchill, his resonant voice growling defiance at the dictators in his broadcasts, the British people were knitted into that magnificent band of brothers they became in 1940. The cynical will stress the fact that it was a common fear, and nothing else, which united us, but unite us it did, and only those who were old enough in 1940 to appreciate what was going on will know what it is like to live in an almost selfless society, proud of its country and all working to a common end. It was a wonderful time to be British.

Chapter 8

The next three weeks were remarkably peaceful ones. The day after the fight with the Dornier we did a short trip escorting a couple of cruisers and a destroyer into the Firth of Forth, and it looked as though they were the last of the many ships that had been out after the *Scharnhorst.* The Army had now been kicked out of Norway and our job settled down to the routine sweeping of the sea between Scotland and Norway. It was at this time that all non-commissioned aircrew were given the rank of Sergeant. Non-commissioned pilots had held the rank of Sergeant for many years but the wireless operators and air gunners held whatever rank they had achieved in their basic trades. The wireless operators were already plying their basic trade but gunners were volunteers from among the other tradesmen of the squadron — fitters, riggers, electricians, armourers, aircrafthands, etc. — who trained in gunnery in peacetime in addition to their normal jobs and who were paid flying pay as a result. They kept up to date with refresher courses and took part in the month's Armament Practice Camp when the squadron went away for intesive training in bombing and gunnery. At these camps the gunners still worked at their basic trades on the aircraft but also did a complete gunnery course, firing the Lewis gun out of the Anson turret just as the pilots did bombing and front firing with the Vickers gun. When the war started the gunners stopped working at their trades and became full-time aircrew.

The crewmen I flew most often with latterly were Corporal Davies as wireless operator and Leading Aircraftman Gilbert as gunner. For the trip on the day after the Dornier fight they appeared self-consciously with their three-bar chevrons on their arms. It was a startling innovation and, for regular servicemen, as the vast majority of us were, it was one that was accepted with reluctance in many quarters. I must admit to having reservations myself but the chief opposition or resentment came, of course, from the old sweats of the Sergeants' Mess, many of them veterans of the Great War and the North-West Frontier of India.

In their mid-forties, with blood thinned by tropical heat, they took a long time to adjust to the nineteen-year-old whipper-snappers who crept fearfully into their holy of holies on that first day. Gradually, of course, the home truth sank in that the whole effort of the station was directed to the sole purpose of getting its aircrew into the air and that, including the pilots, about three-quarters of those aircrew were now Sergeants. After all, however many years an old timer had sweated it out to achieve his rank, it was still the youngster who was the fighting man.

Commissioned gunners had now also made their appearance, one of our first being the unfortunate Dutch Holland who had made that Brock's Benefit night-trip to Hamburg with us and who swore that he was never the same again. He nearly wasn't. He had had a remarkable escape from injury when the 20 mm shell wrecked the wireless set. He'd been standing opposite the set when it went off and bits of wireless set and 20 mm shrapnel flew across the cabin and hit the opposite wall. Not a single piece hit Dutch, though you could almost see the outline of a man on the opposite wall surrounded by pock-marked upholstery.

The peaceful interlude in our lives, about which none of us had any complaint, was quite strange. The North Sea seemed to have emptied of shipping since the German conquest of Norway and, apart from our East Coast convoys, we saw little on our patrols to Norway and back. One incident marred one of the trips for me. I was in the middle of the pre-flight checks but the armourer had not yet appeared with the safety pins from the bombs. These pins ensure that the bombs are safe from accidental discharge on the ground; the armourer unscrews them and hands them to the navigator before take-off. While I knew that the armourer would eventually appear I wished to know whether we were carrying ten 100-pounders or four two-fifties and I asked the fitter to go and have a look into the bomb bay *without* going underneath the aircraft as I didn't want him chopped to pieces by the revolving airscrews. All I wanted to know was whether there were four or ten bombs on the racks so that I could set the Mickey Mouse bombing gear before take-off. (The 'Mickey Mouse' was an automatic machine that dropped the bombs in succession at an interval decided before-hand. In dropping a stick of bombs one dropped the first one as an undershoot and the stick of bombs then followed at your selected interval to run through the target and score a hit, you hoped.) I'd just about finished my cockpit checks when the rigger came rushing up to the cockpit and said that a man was trapped in the bomb doors. A quick squint at the dashboard showed me that the bomb doors were not, indeed, shut as they should have been so I snapped the bomb door lever to 'Open', waited until the tell-tale light showed me that they were, and shut down the engines as rapidly as I could. I joined the rest of the crew under the aircraft to find the fitter I'd sent to count the bomb load lying on the concrete, and he wasn't a pretty sight. He was breathing, which was what mattered most, but his face was purple, his eyes rolled up to the top of his skull and on the sides of his neck were two great, crushed weals where the bomb doors had caught him. By the time the ambulance arrived he was looking distinctly better and a quick call to the M.O. revealed that he would be O.K. so I went off on my patrol, though not very happily, and was much relieved to call in at the Sick Quarters after the trip to find him quite out of danger, though with a neck the size of a submarine's snorkel. I also sorted out with him the cause of the accident.

While only armourers were supposed to remove the safety pins from the bombs and hand them to the navigator the ground crews had, by now, arrived at a co-operative routine whereby they all helped each other. An armourer might turn over an airscrew for a fitter doing an engine check, an electrician waggle the rudders and elevators while a rigger checked the control movements in the cockpit, and so on. The fitter knew quite well that I only wanted to know the number of bombs on the racks, which he could have found out quite easily and safely by just bending down, but he'd decided that he might as well save time and went underneath to start on the job of taking out the safety pins and was caught by the neck when the doors closed on him.

Apart from having the most monstrous and literal pain in the neck he said that the experience wasn't all that bad. I would have thought that death by strangulation would have been extremely unpleasant but he said that he'd been far too busy trying to extricate himself to feel any pain, and this really bore out a conclusion which I had by now reached, that most forms of death are far more merciful than one might imagine. Most of the terror and apprehension in my life had been *before* the action started, in the suspense period, but when the shooting actually started things were much easier as one was completely occupied mentally and physically. First sighting of Messerschmitt 109s in the distance was most depressing and the apprehension grew worse as they closed the range, but as soon as the first gun flashes appeared in their wings and propeller boss then you went into action assessing the best moves to make and you became completely busy and occupied. In the same way this fitter had been far too busy trying to force the bomb doors open again to realise the passage of time and, as far as he was concerned, he was still busily struggling away when he passed out. As a matter of fact he was helped a little in this by the fact that, having opened the bomb doors and put the flaps fully down on my checks, I selected 'Flaps Up' and 'Bomb Doors Closed' together so that when the doors eventually jammed on his neck excess pressure was being bled out of the very powerful hydraulic system both through the jammed bomb-door circuit and also through the flap circuit. If he'd had the exclusive attention of the bomb door circuit I think he may well have ceased to breathe by the time we got on to things.

Another happening during this rather quiet period was an organised Mess party. These were very few and far between now as we were a 24-hour-a-day outfit, really, what with landing late after quitting our operational areas across the North sea and taking off early to get there before dawn. And only a fool did any amount of drinking when you could be called up to immediate readiness at any time of the day or night. Any party would therefore be a fairly muted affair, but a party was a party and much looked forward to. For some reason or other Bill and I seemed to have missed out on the publicity for this party and we landed at about 2230 hours one night to find that the party was the next night and that we would be on another trip at the time. As we didn't want to miss it we found a co-operative all-sergeant crew and swopped duties with them.

We were to get airborne by 0330 hours, which only gave us about a couple of hours in bed before we had to attend briefing. At the appointed time we staggered down to the Ops Room and set off for Norway in the darkness. As soon as we settled down on course the inevitable drowsiness set in and I started to nod off. While the automatic pilot does a very good job it really is advisable to stay awake to keep an eye on him, but I found it becoming more and more impossible. Time and time again I nodded off, to jerk into semi-wakefulness for a few seconds before falling asleep again. As my head jerked up once more into semi-consciousness I suddenly became aware of the surface of the sea flitting past in the light of the exhaust flame of the port engine; we were just about to hit it! I grabbed the wheel and hauled back with all my might. The auto pilot was hydraulically operated and in an emergency one could overcome it by putting enough pressure on the controls to snap the relief valves open. This pressure was quite considerable and when the autopilot gave way it did so suddenly. So my backward heave on the wheel had no effect until the hydraulics gave up the battle suddenly, when the full pressure came on to the elevator and shot us up into a G-laden climb.

The sleeping aircraft immediately awoke and the intercom crackled and squeaked into activity and, as it did so, I realised that the 'sea' that we had nearly hit wasn't the sea at all, but the top of a layer of stratus cloud and that we were still safely at 3,000 feet. It is necessary to realise that the important thing in situations such as this is the maintenance of authority, reputation and good discipline. Little else counts. The queries had ranged from the 'What the hell d'you think you're doing,' from Bill down in the nose (whom I'm prepared to bet was fast asleep himself) to the slightly more respectful, but nevertheless highly suspicious, query from the gunner as to precisely upon *which* bearing, Sir, was the enemy approaching, the query being reinforced by an insolent test-firing of his Brownings. He knew damned well that there wasn't an enemy aircraft within a hundred miles of us — this was well before the days of the night fighter — and there was no point in chucking his weight about in that fashion.

It was obviously time to exert my authority and it was most unfortunate that I heard a voice bleating over the intercom 'Sorry, chaps. Won't occur again. Must have fallen asleep, or something.' Complete silence followed. Bill, I suspected, had already fallen asleep again — after all there wasn't much he could do as we were flying dead reckoning on Met forecast winds and you couldn't see the drink yet to get a drift. Gilbert, in the turret, had obviously acknowledged that the officers always won, so what was the point in wasting more ammunition in protest against his lot? There remained Tubby Davies at the wireless set. Tubby, the unperturbable! I had one ace left up my sleeve, my sandwiches. I handed them over to Tubby hoping that he would accept them as a sacrifice upon my part and not realise that, with my stomach in its normal half-a-meal-a-day existence, it was a relief to get rid of them. 'Sorry, Tubby, it's only bully beef this time.' In the dim glow of his red table lamp Tubby's face lit up. Bully or caviare, it was all the same to him. With not a trace of resentment or insubordination, he unwrapped them and laid into them in a manner which brought the acid back into my stomach. Lucky Tubby!

I opened the side window and, from time to time, stuck my head out to get that wonderful, scalp-tingling massage of the 140-

knot slipstream; anything to stay awake. The gradual lightening of the sky ahead signalled the approach of dawn and the world became light enough for us to start our reconnaissance and to be aware that, just as we could now see, so could we be seen, and the problem of sleeplessness vanished as we came up to the Norwegian coast, turned south for ten miles and then set course for home. There was nothing to report, not a hostile thing in sight, and we were soon clear of any likely danger. The awful lethargy returned. For the next two hours I fought a running battle with sleep and thankfully wheeled the Hudson on to the runway at Leuchars, absolutely dead beat. And the whole thing was to no avail for me. Bill made the party but, by the time I'd got to bed, I dropped into so deep a sleep that the party was over by the time I woke up. They said the female company was something special and Dutch Holland waxed lyrical about them when I saw him down in Flights later in the day, waving his hands sinuously in the air the better to reinforce the pretty basic details he gave us about his particular bird. Sensing my disappointment, he started to console me. 'Now, don't worry, Dopey . . . '
don't worry, Dopey . . . '

'I know, I know,' I broke in, 'Only sparrows can fornicate and fly, but has it occurred to you that I've done quite a deal of flying lately and need a change?

The Luftwaffe had now reorganised since the battle of France and had started bombing attacks on our coastal shipping and ports in the south. It was the opening phase of what was to become the Battle of Britain and the Hurricane and Spitfire squadrons of the home establishment, which Air Chief Marshal Dowding had with prescience and determination kept out of the already lost Battle of France, went into action against them. New names of fighter pilots began to appear in the Press as the actions became daily more numerous, many of them old term-mates from our Flying Training School days, and we all followed with professional interest and pride as we stooged on our routine patrols over the quietening North Sea. Despite the obvious reduction in enemy activity in our theatre I still got that gut-tightening, acid burning in my stomach as we approached the Norwegian coast in scanty cloud cover in case the 109s and 110s appeared to do their cat-and-mouse stuff with us, or the *Scharnhorst* broke out again on a commerce raid. Common sense told one that quite a few Luftwaffe fighter squadrons must have been withdrawn from Norway to back the offensive in the south, but we still had the odd aircraft failing to return from patrol and the most obvious inference was that it had fallen to fighters, the most efficient of the weapons used against us. Morbidly, as we flew eastwards, I dwelled on my unhappy lot yet hoped that the lack of inner resolution, which daily became more difficult to maintain, was not becoming obvious to others, in particular to my own crew and especially to Bill. My standards were not so much slipping as requiring a bigger and bigger effort to maintain, and I hoped that the strain wasn't showing. There was no doubt about it, there wasn't half the joking and skylarking around in the squadron nowadays, the jolly hockey sticks approach to life being virtually non-existent. When I thought of the letter that I wrote to my mother in September 1939, with its '. . . and some fellows have had the luck to meet a German flying boat with whom they had an argument. Both sides did some quite good shooting.' Christ! The grammar might have been correct but how naive could you get? Could I really have felt like that nine months ago? Had it taken only nine months to wear me down to the timid creature that I now knew myself to be, tanking along in my Hudson to help the cause of democracy. Democracy! If we could have democracy without Messerschmitts then I was all for it, but you could stuff the whole concept in its present form as far as I was concerned.

Bill came up on the intercom. 'Alter course three degrees port on to oh-seven-six degrees magnetic.'

I twiddled the autopilot rudder control and flat-turned the aircraft as I called 'Oh-seven-six magnetic it is, Bill.'

It might have helped if Bill showed signs of irresolution, but if he had any such tendency it didn't show much. Anyway, one had to get on with the job; we were still fairly close to our own coastline and it was unlikely that anything was going to happen yet. I carried on with my endless search of the horizon; turn my head fully to the left and sweep slowly forward to dead ahead, then over to the right and sweep forward again. In his turret the gunner would be doing the same in the area astern of us and Bill, between navigating and taking drifts and so on, would add his search in the area ahead of the transparent nose of the aircraft. I alternated with regular checks of the instrument panel, not really checking it instrument by instrument, one just knew by instinct, and quite rapidly, if a needle was out of place. As I lifted my eyes from checking the gyro direction indicator against the magnetic compass the greyness of the horizon seemed, in one place over to port, just that little bit greyer. As the cannon ball increased in weight I took up the binoculars, which confirmed the accuracy of my stomach's forecast.

Ships. And not ours or we'd have them on the plot. I pressed the intercom button. 'Ships, Bill, bearing red oh-four-oh, 15 miles.'

Bill came up the stairs as I turned the aircraft towards them and took over the binoculars. I thumbed the gun button and gave the Brownings a test squirt, Gilbert in his turret following suit.

'Quite a lot of them,' said Bill. 'Can't make them all out but there could be twenty or so.'

'As soon as you've sorted them out get off a quick sighting report, really quick, and we'll go in and give them our load as soon as we can, before they're really alerted,' I said.

Not that it would be all that effective. We were carrying an anti-submarine load of ten 100-pounders, which would be pretty useless against surface vessels. The A-S bomb was a thin-cased bomb with a high charge/weight ratio, the case being just thick enough to withstand impact with the water and it would probably break up on contact with the metal of a ship's hull. Our best chance would be with a near-miss in the water as close to a ship as possible where the bomb would deliver its maximum blast as it was designed to do. Such a near-miss could damage a ship far more than an internal explosion when the bomb casing had already ruptured on impact.

As we got nearer it was obvious that we had a most complicated situation on our hands, there being 19 vessels all told. Six U-boats in line abreast about half a mile apart led the convoy, steering south-west towards England. Behind them, on a slightly different course, were six small vessels that could well have been minesweepers and behind them was a cruiser and six destroyers. It was rather like the sort of exercise they set you at the School of General Reconnaissance — an unlikely assembly of ships on a variety of courses and on an unlikely mission, your job being to compose an accurate and concise sighting report on the situation as quickly as possible. The obvious interpretation in this case was that it was the prelude to an invasion fleet, the minesweepers clearing a channel through our minefields. But, if that was the case, why were the U-boats leading? They would hardly sail into our minefields when there were minesweepers with them who could prepare a safe swept channel. Bill got weaving with the enciphering machine and, when our signal had been acknowledged, I went in on an attack on the nearest U-boat, as I felt that that would be the most profitable target with our existing bomb load. As we got near I whipped open the bomb doors and the spray frothed up along his sides as he opened up his main ballast tanks and crash-dived. It was the first time I'd seen a submarine close up and was keyed up to give him our load of hundred-pounders. Although most people favoured a load of four two-fifties I felt that there was more chance of a hit with ten hundreds and I thought I'd got him cold. As we tore along at full throttle he got lower and lower in the water, his conning tower making a great slick as it sank into the waves and, a couple of hundred yards before we got to him, he slid out of sight, I wasn't worrying. In a few seconds I'd be there and could drop the stick of bombs ahead of his track and it looked as though he was a dead duck.

Incredibly, as we got to his diving position, there was nothing to be seen. Absolutely nothing except the opaque, heaving mass of the North Sea. No slick, no shadowy shape a few feet below the surface, just *nothing* to indicate that somewhere below was a thousand tons of the most deadly and threatening weapon of the war at sea. Bemused by the lack of target I was consoled that there were five more to have a go at and we carried on to the next U-boat, to be faced with the same problem again. And yet again for the remaining four boats; all six went down without leaving a trace of a mark at which to aim our bombs. I was just wondering which of the surface vessels to take on when we sighted a Messerschmitt 110 twin-engined fighter closing in from the other side of the convoy. With its armament of two 20 mm cannon and four machine-guns we were no match for it, having only two guns in the turret with which to reply; we were also 100 mph slower. There was no percentage in bucking that weight of metal so I closed the bomb doors and fled for the nearest cloud cover, about five miles away. I thumbed the gun button yet again, for the third time this flight, and this was only going to leave me about 13 seconds of gunfire in my ammunition tanks. Once in the safety of the cloud we sent off an amplifying report and, as Bill wrestled with the Syko machine it became obvious to me that this could not be the end of the matter. I just couldn't return home and say that a solitary 110 had driven me off. I could visualise the Intelligence Officer lifting his pencil from his pad and saying, 'A 110 drove you away from a convoy. It was *one* 110 you said, wasn't it? Just one?'

It wasn't on.

'Bill,' I said, 'Let me know when you've got that signal off and we'll have another go at them.'

Was I mistaken or did Bill look a bit crestfallen? Maybe he was just busy with the coding. Surely he couldn't feel as craven as I did about things? Quite impossible. Or was it? It would be a relief, really, to know that his courage was ebbing along with mine, but I couldn't really broach the subject because he'd shown no obvious signs of reluctance to engage the enemy so far. I circled unhappily until the second signal had been sent off and acknowledged, then we broke cloud and made off across the cloudless area in which the enemy ships sailed westwards. We settled for a high level attack on the second line of ships — the cruiser and the destroyers — and, as we went in on the bombing run, the customary dialogue of jittery pilot and intent bomb aimer ensued, though Bill did keep on muttering about something strange moving very rapidly over the surface of the sea 5,000 feet below.

'Stop nattering, Bill, and get on with aiming those bloody bombs.'

'That's what I'm trying to do, if only you'd give me a bit of peace. What course and speed shall I set on the bombsight for those destroyers; they're going quite slowly really, convoy-style.'

'Any damned course and speed you like, Bill. We gave 'em 240 degrees at 12 knots on the sighting reports.'

'O.K. 240/12 it is.'

I could nearly hear Bill's brain working as he fussed over his bombsight. We were getting nearer now, but I wished he'd get a move on. 'Bomb doors open, Bill.'

'Keep her as she is,' called Bill. '140 knots indicated, 5,000 feet. Left-left.'

'Tell you what, Bill, I'll turn up the taps a bit; I'll take her in at 165.'

'No you bloody won't, I've got all my settings fixed now. Keep at 140. And I *did* say left-left . . . Left-left . . . Steady . . . Right a bit. Here it comes a-bloody-gain. There's something moving damned fast down there, fairly skipping along.'

'Yes, Bill, hallucinations do.'

The puffs of exploding anti-aircraft shells from the warships started to dot the sky around us, not that it was all that worrying, even in my present jittery state. As long as they were aiming at us we'd be fairly safe but, you never knew, all it needed was some clot to feed the wrong information into the gunnery director and they stood a chance of clobbering us. And there was still that gentleman with his two 20 mm cannon and four guns that I was expecting up my backside any minute now.

'Steady as she is, Dopey . . . Hell, the bastards have increased speed and are zig-zagging; I'll have to reset my enemy speed bar.'

'Do that very thing, Bill. But quick-like.'

'That's fine, that'll cope with it. Right . . . riiiggghhht. Steady.'

'How much longer, for God's sake?'

'Not to worry, Dopey, keep her as she is. But I *did* say 140 knots, not 143,

Bloody cheek!

'Here it comes again.'

'Here *what* comes again . . . I *am* turning right, can't you feel the damned thing skidding? We'll be over Heligoland soon if you don't get a move on.'

'Right a touch . . . riigght. Steady at that . . . Left-left, left-left. Steeeaaaady. Steady. Bombs gone.'

About bloody time too. I shut the bomb doors and turned for home. 'What's all this stuff you've been rabbiting on about, Bill, the fast-moving effort?'

'Damned funny. It's *really* fast, sort of V-shaped, close to the surface. Here it comes again, coming in from the left, just behind the destroyers. Quick, take a look.'

I dipped the left wing down, skidded on a bit of right rudder and looked down between the port engine and the fuselage at the ships below. And then I saw it.

The optician, when he made my glasses, had said that he'd over-corrected them a bit and it looked as though my eyesight with glasses was better than Bill's because there was no mistaking them for what they were. I shoved the throttles through the gate to Emergency Take-off Boost and the airscrews up to full fine. The nearest cloud was dead ahead, thank God. I clicked the intercom on again.

'For Christ's sake, Bill. For the last few minutes you've been looking at five of the best-selling products of the Bayerische Flugzeugwerke A.G. . . . 109s Bill. One oh bloody nines. Five of the sods in Vic formation. You want your head seeing to, taking me over that lot like a sitting duck at my time of life.'

As we looked down in dismay the first of our bombs hit the water near the flight of 109s. Quite obviously the fighter boys had become bored with their convoy escort and had been indulging in a low-flying beat-up of the ships instead of circling round at about our height waiting for intruders. The succeeding line of nine waterspouts from our exploding bombs marched forward towards the line of destroyers, the nearest being about 50 yards away from one ship, but the 109s flew right through them. They couldn't help it and must have given them the shock of their lives.

One second jolly fighter boys cavorting after their leader about 20 feet off the deck and the next in the middle of ten impressive waterspouts, any of which would have shattered an airscrew or broken off a wing, and which made rather a mockery of their entire mission — the defence from attack of their convoy.

They were going to be a very cross bunch of guys and, as they came curving up off the water in a split-arse turn to climb in pursuit, they reminded me of a Walt Disney film I'd seen of a stirred-up wasps' nest. The humour of the situation lasted a full half-second before my stomach went into a knotted-up ball and Bill and I did some rapid mathematics as Gilbert, in the turret, gave his guns a test squirt. To improve my morale I thumbed my own gun button yet again for half a second and the twin Brownings rattled away in the nose and the cordite fumes leaked back into the cockpit.

'What's their rate of climb, Bill? 2,500 feet per minute, d'you think?'

'About,' said Bill.

'That's two minutes to get up to our height, and they can still overhaul us, even on the climb. How far is that cloud bank, Bill?' (I was pessimistic. I thought it was about six miles away, in which case we'd probably had it; we weren't going to last long against five cannon and 20 guns.)

'About five miles, maybe four,' said Bill.

Bless him, always the optimist. If he was right we'd get away with it. With the supercharger boost gauges at an impressive 40 inches of mercury, against the manufacturer's recommended figure of 35½, the engines were getting a bit of a hammering but you didn't have to be an accountant to work out that it was going to be far better to be tucked up in that cloud with two over-strained engines than to be the proud possessor of two engines in perfect condition as you smashed into the drink riddled like a colander.

The 109s, now in echelon formation on their leader, rose up on our port quarter prepared to sweep into successive attacks when they got our height and my stomach appeared to be laying odds that they were going to win but, as they got in to about 400 yards, and still a thousand feet below us, the first wisps of cloud flitted past, then more and more and we finally plunged into that glorious ten-tenths of strato-cumulus, four very relieved people.

Bill disappeared into the nose and came back in a minute or two, holding his sandwiches and thermos flask. 'Steer 286 degrees magnetic, Dopey.' I checked the compass deviation card and stuck on two degrees of correction to 288 degrees compass. 'Two-eight-six magnetic it is, Bill.'

'Sandwich?' asked Bill, handing his pack towards me.

God, how could he do it? I could no more have put food into that leaden , dragging stomach of mine than I could fly this aircraft to the moon. 'No thanks, Bill. Not hungry.'

'Remember the butter and ham from that torpedoed ship?' continued Bill. 'Now those were the days!'

I just had to get him off the subject of food; my stomach was a sea of acid. 'Bill, would you (a) stop talking about food, (b) stop talking with your mouth full, and (c) would you like to borrow my glasses on the next trip. Or I'll buy you a set. Maybe we can have a whip-round the crew for you. After that effort I'm sure they'll be only too pleased to oblige.'

Bill grinned. 'Not to worry, just leave things to me, you'll be O.K.' We slid down below cloud level, had a good look around and flew westwards home.

'I wouldn't like to be those fighter boys when they get back home,' continued Bill. 'I'll bet Goering will come down from Luftwaffe headquarters and personally bury his boot in each of those five arses. They'll end up flying desks for the rest of the war.'

I could well imagine it. And, as I did, the thought arose, 'How nice it would be, really, just to have to fly a desk for the rest of the war. When you came to think about it there were far worse occupations.'

Three days later we did an odd sort of trip about which I have only the haziest recollections. Four Hudsons of 224 Squadron, with Bill and me making a fifth, went off on a shipping strike somewhere off the German coast. Bill and I were the most experienced crew but we didn't lead the flight; I suppose it was a 224 strike, with us dragged along in a barrel-scraping effort to make up an adequate strike force. It being Bill's turn to fly and with us as No.5 there wasn't an awful lot for me to do as navigator except keep a check on our position.

We stooged up and down the German coast looking for our target, which seemed to be an elusive one, flying in pouring rain at times and I was a bit confused about the whole affair as we wandered along, flying far too close for comfort to the German naval base at Heligoland. I was beginning to feel like a leaderless sheep in strange company. I do remember, just after passing Heligoland, in a slashing rainstorm as dusk was falling, looking out of the window as I sat alongside Bill and seeing what looked like three 110s overtaking us only two hundred yards to starboard. In the wretched visibilty I thought there was something a bit strange about them and I wondered if they were Potez 63's (which the French Air Force had) that had been confiscated from the French and pressed into Luftwaffe service. (We'd had some Potez 63's with us at Leuchars early in the war, doing just what, I don't know, and I was vaguely familiar with the aircraft). In the bad flying conditions, whatever the intentions of the fighters, we didn't connect but the avoiding action we took lost us the remaining four aircraft and we stooged on alone. We were just about to pack up when, from out of the darkness and murk flaming onions and pom-pom tracer rose up at us from the sea, followed by heavy ack-ack bursts and it looked as though we had fortuitously lighted on the convoy we were seeking. It was foolish of them to have opened fire as, had they not, we wouldn't have known that they were there, but as it turned out it didn't matter one way or the other. We came round in a circle to attack them but, by this time, night had really fallen and, in the rain and wretched visibility, we couldn't find them and came home, landing in the wee, sma' hours.

The next day, however, we led the strike force, this time against a 10,000 ton tanker which was running into the Skagerrak, escorted by five flak ships. (We found out later that the ship was the *Nordmark,* sister ship of the prison-ship *Altmark* and, like her, a supply ship for commerce raiders. She was on her way back to Germany). Other Hudsons from 220 Squadron at Thornabay had had a crack at it earlier in the day and it was thought that they'd got home with one bomb, but the ship was still sailing when last seen. We led three other aircraft, two from 233 — Ather and Sgt Crabtree in one and Sgt Bailey flying the other — and one from 224 — Morrison and Sgt Cotton. Before we took off we agreed our tactics: to attack in two pairs simultaneously from opposite directions, so as to spread the gunfire. We found the ships and I gave Morrison and Ather five minutes to get around the other side of the convoy. When this time had expired I went in with Sgt Bailey as No.2 on my starboard side, flying at about 1,500 feet. There was a layer of about five-tenths strato-cumulus cloud with a base at 2,000 feet and we would pop-up into this after dropping our bombs.

The usual atmosphere of a bombing run against a well-defended target built up in my skull as we ran in and I wished I'd never heard of Wagner and his damned Valkyries. From the six ships a load of 20 mm and 40 mm hate rose up, the curling smoke of the tracers and incendiaries reaching out to smash the guts out of us. As we rushed in, the *Ride of the Valkyries* ran through and through my head and seemed to dominate everything. Well, not *really* everything. I couldn't shut out the sight of those smoky fingers and winking gun muzzles, and felt aggrieved that it was Wagner's compatriots who were hurling this load of shit at us and anyway, those goddamed Valkries hadn't got to fly a Hudson three hundred miles away from home. And where, when you came to think of it, were Ather and Morrison who were supposed to share this gunfire with us? Half a mile to go and no sight of them coming in from the other side and just *look* at this group of five 40 mm smoke trails; one of them's going to come right through the windscreen marked 'Dopey Edwards' and I suppose bloody Wagner will provide a clash of cymbals as the thing goes off in my face. And if Bill doesn't get rid of those bombs in short order I'm going to give him a piece of my mind pretty soon. Or press the 'Jettison' button on him. That'll show him who's in charge; prissying about with that bloody bombsight of his. Yeah, give him the surprise of his life as he sees the bombs fall away when I press the Jettison. Do him good. Wake his ideas up a bit.

'What's that? I *am* holding her steady. 140 bloody knots at fifteen hundred bloody feet and if you can do better come and have a try. But don't look out of the windscreen, you crazy Kiwi, or it might put you off a bit.'

'Say again. What! Bombs gone. Good old Bill. Good old bloody Bill. Bomb doors shutting, Bill. Try and mark the stick. Sgt Bailey's, too, if you can see them,'

But what on earth's the thud and vibration? And why am I in a screaming climbing turn, and why am I looking down through the roof of Sgt Bailey's cockpit, and why is he looking up at me in such a puzzled way?' And Bill's call of 'One hit' doesn't seem all that important really when you look out of the window and see a white plume of vaporising petrol a foot in diameter streaming away from the underside of the port wing root. We'd been hit by a 20 mil in at least one tank.

I put the Hudson right way up again and Sgt Bailey fell in on my starboard wingtip. Bill and I ran a check on everything. It looked as though we'd lost about a hundred gallons of petrol and, when Bill had finished his calculations, it looked as though we weren't going to get home, but would drop down in the sea about 20 miles from home. Fortunately Sgt Bailey would see where we ditched and we now had Air-Sea Rescue in our patch and were informed that the high speed launch had already left Tayport to fish us out of the drink.

As we settled down on the journey home I brought Gilbert out of the turret when we were safely away from any likely fighter interference as the Hudson trimmed better that way and we might thus save the odd gallon of precious fuel. He stood alongside me or sat on the main spar as he chatted or, horror of horrors, produced his sandwiches and munched happily away at them, the acid biting deeply into my gut at the mere sight of it. Gilly was in a choir in St. Andrews and they had a public performance on that night. He was torn between the fact that he might not (*would* not in my opinion) get to the concert that night if we had to ditch and the genuine desire to ditch as he'd never done it before and was looking forward to the experience. I wish that the expression 'You must be joking' had been invented in 1940 as it far more suited the occasion than the rather stereotyped 'For Christ's sake, Gilbert, you're off you bloody rocker!' which was all that I could dredge out of my limited vocabulary in my combined horror at the idea of ditching and my reluctant admiration for a chap who thought as I might have thought, say, six months ago and who stilled hankered after experiences.

What I was remembering was a flight in a Walrus amphibian a year or two before when we'd alighted on the water in the Tay estuary. In an aircraft with a properly designed planing bottom the impact as we hit the water was no small one; I could still remember it. If I had to ditch this Hudson I reckoned we were in for a far bigger wallop as we hit the sea with our big, pregnant belly. The nose of the Hudson was a perspex cone which was going to shatter as soon as we hit the sea and tons of water were going to be rammed into the fuselage at our seventy-knot landing speed. There would be no evading that yard-wide, seventy-knot torrent of immense strength that would smash into the stairs, some to be deflected sideways at me, the rest to continue into the cabin, where the three crew would have their backs flattened against the bulkhead against the shock of hitting. When the aircraft came to rest after its very rapid deceleration, probably well nose-down and flooded with water, they would have to struggle to jettison the door, which contained the precious dinghy, and get out before we sank. Just how they would get on I didn't know. We knew our dinghy drill but no amount of practice could prepare us for the actual struggle in the swirling mass of the sea that would fill the aircraft so rapidly. I would probably be best off as my exit hatch was immediately above my head. Just so long as they got that dinghy free!

'You know, sir,' broke Gilly into my train of thought, 'after the war I'm going to join a full-time choir and sing all the time.'

He took another bite at his sandwich. The acid ate deeper. The pain in my stomach got worse. My God, did he *have* to eat in front of me. I got my own back.

'Hasn't it struck you, Gilbert, that there's probably no "after the war" for *us*?' Gilly's open face dropped as he turned to me. I'd certainly succeeded in ruining his day. I felt a complete shit, so I fiddled with the autopilot and ran an instrument check as a cover-up. It revealed that we were about to run out of petrol on our third tank, which I intended to run dry as we'd need every drop to get home.

'Gilly, I want you to work the wobble pump soon. When I change tanks.' I took out the autopilot and flew manually. When the engines cut through fuel starvation they would cut irregularly, one before the other, as the fuel lines were of different lengths, depending on which tank you were on, and the aircraft would react accordingly. I called up Bill and Tubby Davies to warn them of the impending, but only temporary, loss of power. The starboard engine lost revs and back-fired.

'*Now,* Gilly. Pump like hell!'

Gilly worked the fuel pump handle to and fro as I changed over to our last fuel tank, itself only half full. The Hudson yawed to the right and I stuffed the nose down to keep up the airspeed, and eased on left rudder. The port engine spluttered and we swung left as it died so I brought the rudder back to central, then the starboard engine started to get its fuel and it banged and stuttered its way back to full power as I put on right rudder to counter it. The port engine came on song and we were straight and level again, with just a 200-foot loss of height. But still that damned westerly wind. I re-engaged the autopilot and checked our fuel. About 60 gallons. Just less than an hour's flying at cruising revs. I called Bill up on the intercom. 'What's our ETA, Bill?'

'We'll be home in an hour,' said Bill cheerfully. 'Call it 1630. How's the juice?'

'Oh, so-so, Bill. We might get our feet wet.'

I pushed the carburettor mixture controls even further forward, then a bit more, to weaken the mixture and so save fuel. The cylinder head temperatures went well into the red. Bill came up the stairs.

'Yes, I've checked our ETA again, about 1630. Jesus, you're running the engines a bit hot, aren't you? Look at those cylinder head temperatures!'

'Bugger the cylinder head temperatures,' I replied.

'If you say so,' said Bill, and we flew silently on.

He broke the silence. 'Tell you what', he said, 'I'll just go and check that the carrier pigeons are O.K.'

'Good idea. And get a message all ready for ditching so that you can just fill in time and position before you let the bird go. And try and bring the other two birds with you into the dinghy.'

'Land ahead,' said Gilbert some time later.

The coast of Fife came up and a check on our fuel gauges resulted in smiling faces all round, even Gilbert's.

'Well, Gillie, I hope you're in good voice for the Hallelujah chorus tonight, I'm sure they'd have missed you if we'd dropped in the drink.'

I wheeled the Hudson on to the runway and ran onto the tarmac, as the aircraft would have to go into workshops for the kind of repairs which we were going to need. We all clambered out and, as we looked at the damage, we realised how lucky we'd been. You could put your head through the hole in the base of the wet-wing tank, which held 143 gallons when full. I'd checked its contents before we ran in on the bombing run and it held 100 gallons, which left a 40-gallon airspace above the petrol. We'd been hit by a 20 mm explosive cannon shell, which has a very slightly delayed-action fuse so as to allow the shell to penetrate the skin of the aircraft before exploding. In this case the shell had obviously exploded within the 100 gallons of petrol, where there was no free oxygen, so no explosion or fire had resulted. Had it gone on just those few extra inches into the vapour space the resulting explosion would probably have blown the wing off.

At the de-briefing Sgt Bailey said he thought that one of his two-fifties had gone home also, so it looked as though we'd done the ship a fair amount of damage. But the other two aircraft didn't return so the 50 per cent casualty rate was a depressing debit. The obvious assumption was that Ather and Morrison had been jumped by fighters on the far side of the convoy, no anti-aircraft weapon being as efficient as the fighter. It was a sobering thought and one more step in the erosion of my morale.

The next week we did five routine patrols without incident but, thankful though I was for the lack of action, I did an awful lot of thinking, the feeling of depression weighing more heavily on me each time I flew. If the next shipping strike, which couldn't be all that far ahead, produced 50 per cent casualties again then the luck had to run out some time. And that had been only against a tanker escorted by flak ships and, presumably, a few fighters. The last time the *Scharnorst* had broken out the Hun had put 30 to 40 fighters over her all the time as an umbrella as she sailed up the Norwegian coast, and you didn't last long against that sort of opposition; certainly Feeney and Andy Wallis had only a few minutes before they went flaming down into the North Sea. I just hoped that the end would be quick and almost wished that it would come, just so long as it was sudden, without too much cat-and-mouse stuff. And then everlasting peace! And, my God, talking about peace, hadn't we changed since those days only ten months ago! What price the pseudo motto which used to hang over B Flight office door — '*Semper in Excreta*' ('Always in the shit'). And that Army recruiting poster that someone had acquired which stated in bold lettering 'Join the Army and see the World', beneath which some wag had written equally bold 'Join the Air Force and see the Next.' That poster had come down now and had been replaced by a more apposite one showing a hazy 109 almost invisible against the flaming ball of the sun. 'Beware of the Hun in the Sun' it advised.

I took a look at the sea. Judging by the wind lanes it looked as though the wind was backing as we flew westwards home so I got down to the bombsight and took a drift, which had altered with the change of wind. I called up Bill. 'Alter course 3 degrees port to 258 degrees magnetic. Land fall Peterhead, ETA four minutes late.'

The aircraft skidded as Bill twiddled the autopilot, and settled down on her new course. I wondered if I'd be able to eat dinner tonight. I was feeling mighty hungry as I'd laid off all day and was looking forward to a good tuck-in but I'd been caught out so often before. Usually it took only about five minutes into the meal before that burning feeling came up but one really had to eat sometime and often I'd ignore the pain or, rather, say a mental 'to hell with it,' and carry on eating, knowing that the damned thing would win; it couldn't be beaten or hadn't been so far. Then off to my room for a blaspheming hour or two waiting for it to subside and swearing I wouldn't eat so much next time, promise I won't, just so long as it would go away soon. But it always took its time about it.

The intercom came to life. 'This ETA correct, Dopey?'

'Yes, Bill, only one more hazard ahead.'

'Hazard! My God, what's that?' Did I detect a note of jumpiness?

'Yes, Bill, the landing. After that last effort of yours I had hiccups for half an hour.'

'Oh, *very* funny, quite the humorist!'

'One tries, Bill, one tries. Anyway, allowing 30 seconds for bounces, we should finally be on the deck by 2050.'

Which we were. To find a message in the Flight office to the effect that all four members of the crew were to report to the Medical Officer in Sick Quarters in the morning, which was a bit odd. In peace time medicals had been regular and strict, everyone laying off the beer for a week before them, running round the aerodrome and all that sort of thing, all ideas of emulating the versatile sparrow that could both fornicate and fly being dropped for the week so that we could enter the medical in tip-top form. Since the war had started there had been no mention of medicals, which was fair enough, I suppose. After all, with a war on your hands you weren't going to encourage chaps to go sick. If we were going to have medicals tomorrow they would test my vision, and a sense of lightness pervaded my being at the thought that inevitably they would find out that I was short-sighted and that they would automatically ground, me. But say they didn't do the eye tests? I wondered if, somehow, I could arrange to drop my glasses case onto the floor as I took out my handkerchief, or something like that, just to make sure they copped me. But, as I looked at Bill stowing his parachute into his locker, the depression returned because I knew it just wasn't on. Physically Bill looked as fit as a flea and hadn't any easy let-out that I knew of and the old conviction returned: if you didn't do your job properly some other chap had to go out later and do it for you, I was back in the machine.

Next morning Bill and I went to Sick Quarters. I was in first. 'Morning, Doc.'

'Morning, Dopey. Have a seat, will you. Just want a chat. How're you feeling?'

'Adequate, Doc.'

'How many operational hours have you done, any idea?'

What an odd question for an M.O. to ask! 'Not absolutely sure, Doc. About five hundred, maybe five-fifty. I could find out from my log book if you need to know.'

'No, that'll be accurate enough for my purpose. Now, how are you eating nowadays, any trouble?'

How on earth did *he* know? 'Well, a bit, but I don't eat all that much, really.'

'What did you have for breakfast?'

'Didn't have any, Doc. Thought I'd save it up for lunch.'

'Why?'

'Less discomfort that way. And my family run to fat and I

don't want to follow in the tradition.'

But the Doc wouldn't let it go and, as the inquisition went on, I must say that I was starting to enjoy it. Like all shy people I was basically a confirmed egotist and, once we'd slipped into the routine of discussing me to the exclusion of all else, I found that I was well at home with the fascinating subject.

'How would you like a holiday?' asked the Doc later.

'You mean, a spot of leave, Doc?'

'Not exactly. Two or three weeks doing nothing in a convalescent home.'

'You mean like Rossi Priory?'

Rossi Priory had been an experiment to give aircrews a few days' local leave in peaceful surroundings. A country house in Perthshire, its owners had volunteered to take in a few people at a time, the idea being that we would relax in its tranquil atmosphere. The owners were charming and understanding people but I don't think the experiment worked because of that peculiarity of RAF existence, which I mentioned before, whereby you could be fighting for your life at one time and, only a few hours later, be surrounded by all the luxury and safety of civilian life. The incessant mental shuffle was difficult to adjust to. However big a line you shot to a civilian it was impossible for him to grasp the realities of air warfare, true sympathy and understanding being possible only between people of equal experience, and they hadn't had it. There was no doubt but that we were a difficult bunch of people to cater for and we were probably happiest among ourselves. (Four years later there was no such problem in Burma. We were all so far from home and in a 100 per cent service atmosphere that life progressed routinely, no shuttling to and fro to jazz you around mentally.)

'No, not like Rossi Priory. A convalescent home, an Army one, actually. You see, those of you who've been flying since September are going to have a rest from operations. You'll go to the convalescent home for a few weeks and then get posted to a training unit, for example, for a few months before returning to an operational squadron again.'

Incredulous relief and joy surged warmly through me. No more Ops for a while? No more red-winking guns and tracer smoke as you rushed in at the ship with your bomb doors opening? No splintery crashes as the bullets went through the fuselage? No cannon ball in the stomach at the first sighting of the 109s? No pressure wave puffing in eyes and cheeks as the 20 mil went off within the cabin? And what about three meals a day, eh?

What about that? Perhaps even the dream would go. Compounded of a mixture of my crash into the River Eden and Bill's near-miss on the St. Andrews beach after our night-bombing trip to Hamburg it was always the same and came with increasing regularity. With its nose in the air the Hudson was fully stalled and sinking rapidly into the estuary. Endlessly it sank as my stomach, with its customary cannonball, floated up on the weightlessness of the stall, the Valkyries pounding away in my skull, the volume rising and rising as they put their throttles right through the gate as the hellish stall got even worse. The brass pounded, the violins shrilled and worked up to that dreadful, but welcome, CRASHHHH of the cymbals that came just before we hit the estuary and to which I always woke up, sweating and panting, my stomach a contracted ball of pain. Was all this really going to end?

'Christ, Doc. You really mean that?'

'Yes, Dopey, pukka gen.'

'When does it start?'

'In two or three days, when we can arrange it.'

Two or three days! A lot could happen in two or three days. *Scharnhorst* could break out; you could get jumped by 109s; you could hit a hill in bad weather, an engine could cut on take-off.

'The scheme starts now,' continued the Doc. 'You can hang around for a few days while we sort things out. Quite a few of you are going so it'll take a day or two to arrange it.'

'You mean, Doc, I don't fly again?'

'Not operationally, anyway.'

I left the M.O.'s office and bumped into Bill outside. 'You'll never guess what the M.O's got up his sleeve for you, Bill, but I'm sure you're going to like it,' I told him as he went in.

Yet, as I walked back to the Mess, there was the vaguest uneasy feeling that I was running away from my responsibilities, that there was more than a trace of cowardice in my make-up. Still, a rest would be a nice change. '*Nice change!*' What an understatement! It was going to be great. It was good to be alive. Weren't the birds singing loudly? It was great. Wasn't the sun shining beautifully today? Must be first sunshine we've had for weeks. Christ, it was wonderful! Boy, oh boy, what a wonderful world!

Before lunch a fair-sized group of us were nattering contentedly about our future mostly with pints in our hands, but also in a reasonably subdued manner as the majority of people in the Mess weren't in our fortunate position. Those pilots who'd joined early in 1940 still had some time to go before they would be due for a rest and the later replacements we hardly knew. We couldn't flaunt our good luck too obviously in their faces; we were safe and they could be dead tomorrow. There was no doubt about it, we all had something of a guilt complex and it was a relief, a few days later, when a bunch of us from both squadrons climbed into the back of a three-tonner and were driven over to Dunbavin Hydro, about 30 miles away, where we joined up with other crews from 269 Squadron at Wick and 220 from Thornaby, our old peace-time station way back in '37. The Hydro had been taken over by the Army as a convalescent home and it seemed a pity that every carpet had been stripped out of the place, so that one clanked everywhere on bare boards through its Spartan corridors. Still, we weren't grumbling; we had our own rooms, there was an indoor swimming pool and there was nothing to do except laze around. We weren't medical cases; we were obviously using up vacant space as a convenient way of giving us our carefree rest so we didn't come into contact with the medical staff of the hospital, we messed with the administrative Adjutant in two rooms, an ante-room and a dining room.

Captain McClibborn, the Adjutant, had been in the '14-'18 war and I early sensed that he viewed us with an element of contempt; after all, there wasn't a bullet wound between the lot of us. I found his critical attitude difficult to cope with as my inner guilt feeling backed up his more overt stance. McClibborn was superficially cordial and full of a spurious bonhomie that made me want to wriggle when he was at his most effusive and aroused in me an unfortunate lack of desire to look him in the eye so that I suspected he thought me a shifty character, as well as being of craven make-up. He was assisted by an unfortunate young Lieutenant Elphinstone from a Highland regiment whose sole job seemed to be that of Soldiers' Welfare Officer. Just what misfortune of posting had winkled Elfie out of a fighting unit to do a piddling job like this I can't imagine but 1940 was, of course, a strange and unsettling time for the Army. Having been kicked out of the only two toe-holds we had on the continent of Europe — France and Norway — it was to be some time before the British Army actually fought the Wehrmacht, only the Navy, Merchant Navy and Air Force being in contact with the enemy. Units had straggled back from Norway and Dunkirk decimated in numbers and with few weapons except their rifles, and a tremendous job of reorganisation was in hand. I suppose poor

Elfie's name had just come out of the hat to be Welfare Officer at Dunbavin Hydro, so there he was.

Used, as we all were, to the informality and friendliness of an RAF mess we failed at first to understand the way in which McClibborn pulled rank and held Elfie at arm's length; never friendly and always addressing him as 'Mr', until it became obvious that the real reason for the attitude was that Elfie was a nephew of the Queen. Of reasonably lowly background, McClibborn was making it quite clear to everyone that, Queen's nephew or not, a captain was a captain and a lieutenant a mere lieutenant. He was horrid to Elfie as often as he could be but I don't suppose that Elfie's sufferings lasted too long; I'm sure he'd have been back with his unit within a month or two.

The hot August days drifted pleasantly past for us as the aerial fighting that was to become known as the Battle of Britain gained momentum. The newspapers and radio news reports were full of the fighting and familiar names of former term-mates of our Flying Training School days made national headlines as the Hurricanes and Spitfires tore into the enemy formations and shot down the Dorniers, Heinkels and Messerschmitts. Superficially, certainly, it looked as though we were doing well, then the Luftwaffe shifted its targets from the ports and shipping and started to attack our fighter squadron bases, while the proportion of fighters to bombers in the invading armadas was heavily increased. I don't suppose that anyone in England really visualised defeat and, in common with many, we found ourselves thinking of the opposing rates of destruction of aircraft in a way analogous to the cricket scores. At breakfast each day one tended to ask what the scores were until the continuous repetition brought home to us as pilots the fact that this was not, indeed, a cricket match but a slogging battle in which the fighter boys were dying and being worn down just as we had been. Captain McClibborn made it amply clear, by his effusive praise of the fighter boys, that the place for a pilot in any war was in his cockpit, not lounging around a comfortable convalescent home. His barbs sank in; we did, indeed, feel guilty. But we also didn't feel like going to war again.

I decided to get away and managed to borrow an autocycle and some petrol coupons. Armed with my ration card, and with my emptied gas mask case stuffed with the minimum of kit, I puttered away in the general direction of the Western Highlands and revelled in the peaceful and impressive scenery. To my great disappointment, on the second day the engine of the autocycle seized up due, I suspect, to the fact that some garage must have put neat petrol into the tank of the two-stroke machine instead of a petroil mixture. Sadly I wheeled the machine to the nearest railway station and settled down to a wait of several hours. As the train drew in I put the autocycle into the guard's van and clambered into a compartment to find that one of the two occupants was an ex-Medical Officer from Leuchars, the other being a drinking pal of his. From the flying boat base at Oban the two of them were coming to Stirling to spend a 48-hour leave whooping it up. As they were equipped with the standard travelling pack of a bottle of whisky each, which they generously shared with me, the journey soon became a very pleasant one. The compartment was of the non-corridor type with its own toilet, a pleasantly self-contained unit, and the noise level was becoming such that any traveller opening the door at the numerous stops rapidly changed his mind, slammed the door and sought a more peaceful journey in another compartment, which suited us alright. The other two drank from glasses which they'd brought with them and, after a while, the Doc's training in hygiene got the better of him in that he began to disapprove of the fact that I had to swig directly from the bottles. He ingeniously solved the problem by unscrewing one of the glass lamp shades, fishing in his medical bag and finding a large pill box whose lid he sealed to an open end of the lamp glass with adhesive plaster. It was a completely successful operation and a most useful one for me as, the glass being opaque, neither of my benefactors could see just how large a measure I was taking each time. Such a spontaneous party had the inevitable result that we all got gloriously tight in a real, happy RAF binge. We reverted, alas, to type and dredged up from our memories those half-forgotten dirty songs that I don't think I'd sung for a couple of years, at least.

'The donkey is a queer bloke,' sang the Doc in his quite nice, if somewhat powerful voice,

'And very seldom gets a poke,
But when he does he lets it soak,
As he revels in the joys of copulation.'

The Engineer Officer and I struck up the chorus.

'Cats on the roof tops, cats on the tiles,
Cats with syphilis, cats with piles,
Cats with their arseholes wreathed in smiles
As they revel in the joys of copulation.'

We followed with '*The Cruise of the Good Ship Venus*' but, before we could finish, a hammering on the wall indicated the displeasure of the occupants of the adjoining compartment and we were forced to cool it a bit. The Doc, contrary to all my naive preconceptions of the standards of behaviour of that noble profession — Hippocratic Oaths, General Medical Councils and all that sort of stuff — was not only exceedingly fond of women but appeared to regard his peacetime practice chiefly as a recruiting ground for bedmates, and had a very practical approach to the matter.

'You see, Dopey, it's a great help being in the profession,' he said, belching whisky fumes complacently. 'When you consider that every woman who walks into my surgery is going to take her knickers off at some time or other, well, it's a bit of a pushover, isn't it?'

I was forced to agree and regretted that it did not appear necessary for the WAAFs with whom I came in daily contact — the MT drivers, clerks, cipher officers and so on — to remove their knickers in order to carry out the duties assigned to them. I was evidently in the wrong job.

The train decanted three well-intoxicated RAF types on to the platform at Stirling, the other two being met by their paramours with a car. The Doc had described the physical charms of his bird in the minutest detail and I had not, hitherto, appreciated the subtle nuances that such-and-such an anatomical attribute could introduce into the very athletic style which the Doc evidently favoured. He liked his women thin and gave convincing reasons for his preference.

'Here come our tarts,' said the Doc. There was no need to ask which one was his. Despite the Doc's learned, and most convincing, exposition of the advantages of thin women I retained at that moment, as I still do, a preference for females with more meat on 'em.

'Their husbands are on night shift,' explained the Doc. 'Pity there's not a third one for you.'

Had there been one of more pneumatic type I would have been inclined to agree with him but, at that moment, the guard thrust the useless autocycle into my hands and abolished whatever sexual fantasies which might have been stirring in my brain. I gazed fairly enviously after the quartet as the women supported their men to the car. For me there merely remained a five-mile push with my seized autocycle, a physical effort that did much to evaporate the almost neat whisky which was circulating in my veins.

I rejoined the mob at breakfast and we got up-dated on the latest Battle of Britain scores. Captain McClibborn was on form, and I think that it must have been about this time that Nicolson got his Victoria Cross, the only one awarded to a Battle of Britain pilot. (Was it only three years since I'd nearly hit Nic's Fury in a whirling maelstrom of aircraft in the biggest near-accident in the RAF's history, when 24 Hart and Fury biplanes got into a muddle at Tern Hill. It seemed a long time ago, when I was very young.) McClibborn gave Nic the full admiration treatment, the inference being that the present company could obviously not match up to that sort of courage or, even if they could, they could hardly prove the point by lounging around a convalescent home while their friends were daily locked in combat against formidable odds. We ate in silence until McClibborn left the table. Then one of us, perhaps a little more resilient than the rest, muttered 'I'll bet that bastard never even saw a trench in the '14-'18 affair. I'll lay odds he spent his time cleaning out the bogs at Skegness.'

Most of us silently agreed but, at lunch, McClibborn really scored an ace. Half-way through the meal he announced that he had received a signal about us. 'Well, gentlemen, you are all returning to your units on Thursday. A medical officer is coming from 18 Group Headquarters tomorrow to see you all.'

A stunned, horrified silence followed. We dared not look at each other in case the shame showed. I looked unseeingly at my plate as the cannon ball dragged down my stomach.

'But we were promised a three-month rest,' came a quiet protest from someone. 'We were *promised*'

'I can't help that, I'm sure,' said McClibborn in a satisfied tone. 'Will you all be ready to see your M.O. from 1000 hours tomorrow onwards?'

He chomped solidly through the rest of his food and left the Mess. Elfie got up to follow him. 'Bad luck, chaps,' he said as he went.

'Thanks, Elfie.'

This was worse, I thought, than if we'd never had this carefree rest. Why, oh why, had they pulled this one on us? It would have been far better to have left us as we were, just expecting to go on flying, than to show us the light and then slam the door on us like this. A morose and miserable body of men dispersed from the Mess, chiefly alone. I walked towards Stirling then gave it up and turned back for Dunbavin, to meet Tubby Davies and Gilbert, my wireless operator and gunner, on a similar outing.

'Have you heard the news, chaps?' I asked them.

They nodded. 'We got it in the Sergeants' Mess at lunch time.'

As we walked back to Dunbavin no words like fear, fright, terror, cowardice, death, apprehension or misery were mentioned, and certainly not courage; we all skated around the point, not one of us bold enough to come out into the open with the fact that, however brave a body of men we had been in September 1939, we certainly didn't measure up to those standards now.

In the morning the Medical Officer arrived and interviewed us. It was quite an informal affair, sitting out on the grass in the sunshine and chatting away to him as he made a few notes on his pad.

'Right, Edwards, that's fine,' he said. 'You'll go back to you unit on Thursday pending posting to a training job.'

Had I heard him alright? 'Posting, sir? Training job?'

'Yes, I thought you all knew about it before you came here. You'll get about three months rest before you rejoin an operational unit but there hasn't been time to sort out all your postings so you'll have to go back to your units and hang around for a while. No operational flying, mind you, you're not to do that.'

'No, sir, of course not.' I hoped my grin did not show. *Three* months, just think of it! I'd see my 22nd birthday.

'But you'll have to keep an eye on that ulcer of yours,' said the Doc. 'Avoid greasy foods as much as you can.'

'Ulcer, sir, what ulcer?'

'You've got an incipient duodenal ulcer.'

'What on earth's that?'

'No time to go into details but, if you watch your diet it ought to clear up fairly soon. Lay off the alcohol, too, it doesn't do an ulcer all that good.'

Never a rose without a thorn! But who cared! Three months with not a 109 or armoured ship in sight; a tracer a chap who worked in a drawing office; perhaps Pimms No.1 on Sunday mornings; bad weather a time to stay on the ground and flying a pleasure. Give me a twin-engined aircraft now and I'd roll it for you. Give me a single-engined job and I'd do a flick roll off the top of a loop.

Next day transport arrived to take us back to our units and we were sent on a fortnight's leave. On my return to the squadron my posting still hadn't been sorted out but I was still commanding B Flight and felt my position acutely as I organised the youngsters' flying details while remaining safely on the ground myself. I frigged away the time doing air tests of aircraft coming off inspection and, one day, a few of us flew across to Abbotsinch on the Clyde, to go aboard the battleship *Revenge.* I was fascinated by the enormous 15-inch guns that she carried as main armament but puzzled by the accumulation of red, scaly rust inside the unprotected muzzles. I must have wondered audibly about this as the Petty Officer showing us round explained that the first shot blew all the shit out of the barrels and then they were back to normal; but to me it seemed a hell of a way to treat a gun. The ship bristled with 20 mm Oerlikons but the most impressive looking anti-aircraft weapons were the 'Chicago Pianos' — the eight-barrelled Vickers pom-poms — that dished out two-pound shells. Few aircraft survived a hit from a two-pounder and I felt sorry for any Luftwaffe pilot having a go at this ship.

We flew back to Leuchars and landed to learn that there had been no Luftwaffe activity over England while we'd been laying into the gin on *Revenge* and, as day succeeded day, the inactivity continued and it looked as though the Battle of Britain was over.

At last my posting to a Navigation School came through and I could leave my present impossible appointment as non-flying Flight Commander. The old peacetime custom of a send-off party in the Mess had vanished with the war, of course, as we were needed to fly at any time of day or night, and I made my farewells in the Mess that night as best I could. I was catching a train at about 1100 hours, a decent time of day when the Mess would be empty and I could creep away without further embarrassment, a kind of rat deserting a sinking ship. I rang the Transport Section to confirm that a fifteen hundredweight would be collecting me and taking me to the station.

'I'll just check that, sir,' said the Flight Sergeant. 'Yes, here it is: Flying Officer Edwards, three-tonner, 1030 at the Officers' Mess.'

'Three-tonner, Chiefy, you must be mistaken, a fifteen hundredweight will do.'

'No, sir, it's a three-tonner that's been ordered. It'll be there at 1030.' Ah well, it seemed rather large, but it would do.

On time, the Albion turned up at the Mess and my batman put my luggage into the back as I climbed up into its high cabin. No one had seen me go, for which I was grateful, as I left them to carry on their war. How things had changed in the last five months, since we had all met those Heinkel 115s off the Norwegian coast on 5 April. No. 233 was a very different squadron now, hardly recognisable as the unit which had started the war. A lot of chaps had gone — Robinson and Godfrey, Mike Clarke and his second pilot, whose name I couldn't even remember now, Evans, McLaren, Yorke, Feeney, our second-in-command, Wallis, Dunn, Wicht, Ewing, Buchanan, Horan, Paton and Immelman, Sgts Hallam, Bousfield, Ather, Crabtree and Cotton. I couldn't remember them all. And as many from 224 Squadron. Then double the number because a wireless operator and gunner went down with each aircraft as well. That was a lot of dead comrades. It hadn't been an Agincourt, this campaign in Norway, but perhaps we *could* call ourselves 'We few, we happy few, we band of brothers.' We wouldn't be able to strip our sleeves on Crispin's Day and show our scars because we had none to show; they were all inside, and no latter-day Shakespeare was going to write us up anyway. But a bond had been forged between those of us who had survived. Despite, probably because of, the stupidity of war; the cruelty and pain, the bereavement, fear and dread; the summoning up of the resolution necessary to do our job, the overcoming of one's fear of letting the other chap down as one rushed at a heavily protected target with the wing men weaving and dodging the tracer trails, had created this rapport between those of us who had survived and with all other fighting men who had faced similar dangers. It was obtainable in no other fashion; it was unique, and was to last for the rest of our days.

I derived some comfort from the fact that, now that we no longer contended the mainland of Norway with the Hun, much of the heat had come off our area of the North Sea and that things were going to be a lot easier for the squadron from now on, and it was only to be a three-month rest, anyway.

The driver was speaking. 'What?'

'We're here, sir, Leuchars Junction.'

'Oh yes. Thanks Corporal. Give me a hand with my kit, will you?' He grinned as we walked round to the back of the truck and swung down the tailboard and the reason for the three-tonner became obvious; the back of it was full of 233 Squadron types and a few 224 as well. It looked as though all the off-duty pilots were there. They jumped down, grinning and slapping me on the back.

'We just came along to make sure you hadn't pinched the Mess silver, old horse,' one said. In a chattering band we pushed and jostled on to the platform and eventually the Edinburgh train came in. A compartment door was opened, bodies swarmed in and stowed my kit and they shoved me in after it. I let down the window and tried to say something appropriate to the noisy mob of well-wishers but it was pretty impossible to have coherent communication. I managed to bellow a 'So long, Bill' to Bill Tacon. I'd come a long way with Bill, and he'd never once let me down. I hoped I'd done as well by him.

The train pulled away and I kept my head out of the window until they receded into the distance. As I pulled the window up and sat down I realised that the only other occupant of the compartment was an attractive young woman sitting opposite me. I thought that I must have been treading all over her toes, or something, during the last few minutes as she was looking at me in an odd sort of way.

And then I realised that my eyes were full of tears and that I couldn't stop them and could only think 'How nice of them to come and see me off like that. How damned *nice*.'

I hid behind my paper and, eventually, started to read it. Yet again there had been negligible air activity over the South of England. It really looked as though the Battle of Britain was over. How relieved those fighter boys must be! Probably they'd be getting a rest too, just like us. Maybe the Hun *had* thrown us out of France and, now, Norway but it looked as though we'd held them to a draw in the Battle of Britain. We'd be back!

Appendix 1

Deflection Shooting

As any sporting shot will tell you it is necessary to aim ahead of a target moving across your front in order to hit it. In the case of an aircraft it takes about a quarter of a second for a .303 machine-gun bullet to travel out to the normal 200-yard combat range. In that time an aircraft travelling at right angles across your front at 200 mph will travel 73 feet. Your gunsight is designed to assist you in aiming that 73 feet ahead. Basically the gunsight for fixed, forward-firing guns (in which the whole aircraft has to be aimed at the target) was a 100 mile-an-hour sight, either the old-style metal ring-and-bead which we had in our Hudsons or the more sophisticated reflector gunsight of the fighter aircraft. When we looked through our sight, keeping both eyes open, we lined up the front bead in the small centre ring of the rear sight and, if the target was crossing at right angles at 100 mph, we aimed our aircraft so that the target was flying directly towards the centred bead and fired as his engine or cockpit cut the outer ring (Fig.1). If he was flying at 250 mph then you lead him by 2½ ring radii (Fig.2). Thus the two sight pictures are correct for 90 degree crossing shots:-

Fig.1.
100 mph

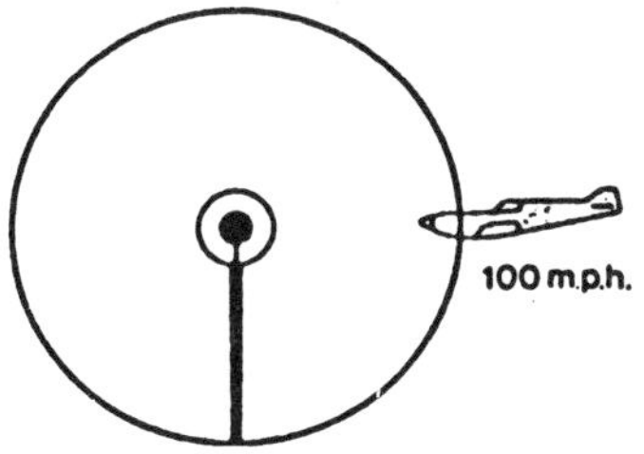

Fig.2
250 mph

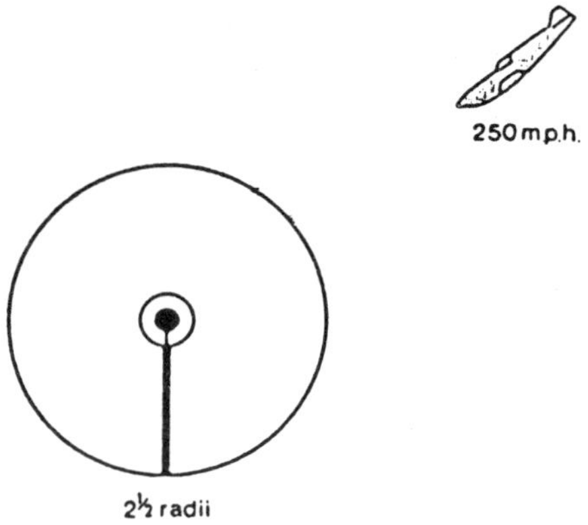

The difficulties of deflection shooting arise because you do not know the exact enemy speed or the angle at which he is crossing your line of sight — the 'angle off', as it is called. From your knowledge of enemy aircraft you have a rough idea of his speed and you have to estimate his angle off by his appearance — foreshortening of profile, the angle when his wing tips begin to appear ahead of his nose, relative positions of rudders, engines, etc. The target has a pronounced tendency to make the shot as difficult as possible by twisting and turning (towards the attacker if he is wise, so as to increase the amount of deflection required) and by altering speed, skidding, etc. to throw you out in your calculations.

If the angle off is 45 degrees then a spot of mathematics will tell you that you give him about 70 per cent of the 90 degrees deflection; at 30 degrees off he will get half. So a chap travelling at 300 mph at 30 degrees off gets the same deflection as one travelling at 150 mph at 90 degrees off — 1½ rings. (Fig. 3.)

Fig. 3

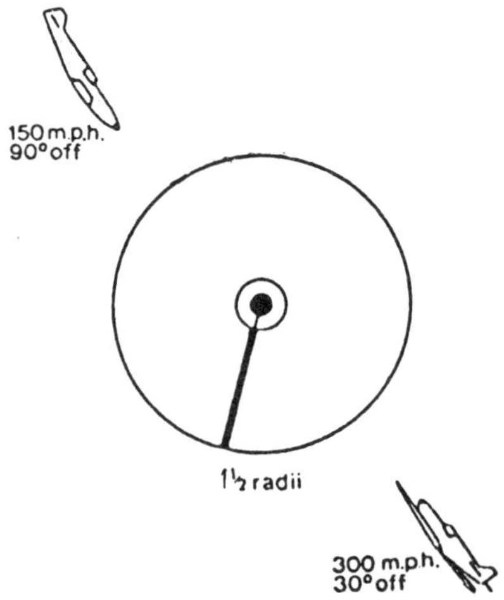

What should be apparent from the sight pictures is that, especially at high target speeds and angles off, you are really 'shooting into thin air' for much of the time. Even if you have estimated the correct number of rings deflection to give the target, you have still to ensure that it is flying directly towards the centre bead. You might well consider that the lower aircraft in Fig. 3 is not quite doing this. In which case you've missed.

From the foregoing you will appreciate that to estimate the correct deflection for a target crossing at 53 degrees off at 237 mph might be difficult. As I have said, the target is rarely a steady one but, even if it flew straight and level at a known speed, if you start you attack at right angles (i.e when he's 90 degrees off) you have progressively, and fairly rapidly, to put on bank to turn with him and to keep pointing ahead of him to keep up the correct deflection. As the attack proceeds this deflection reduces as the angle off diminishes and you end up astern of him firing a nil-deflection shot, which is the ideal shooting position, of course. The angle at which you have to bank your own aircraft in order to turn with the attack increases rapidly until the final stage where you are almost dead astern of the target, when you have to roll off bank rapidly to end up behind him and flying level as he is. The following four illustrations give an idea of the sight picture during the progress of an attack from the beam on a target doing 200 mph. The angle of bank of the attacking aircraft can be seen from the angle the sight pillar makes with the vertical.

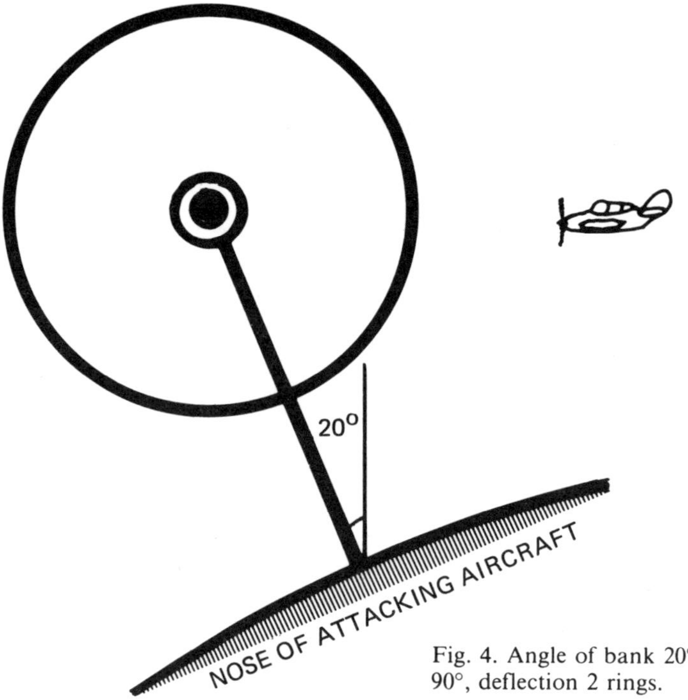

Fig. 4. Angle of bank 20°, angle off 90°, deflection 2 rings.

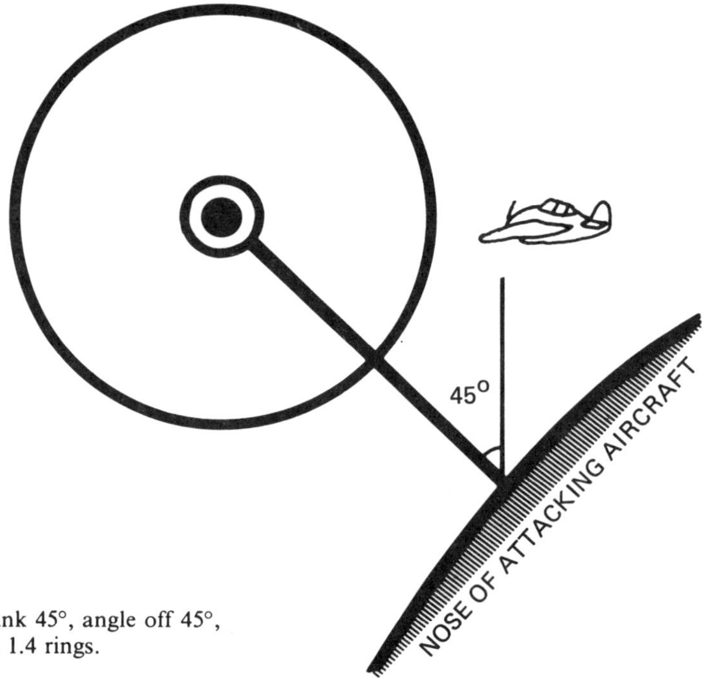

Fig. 5. Bank 45°, angle off 45°, deflection 1.4 rings.

Fig. 6

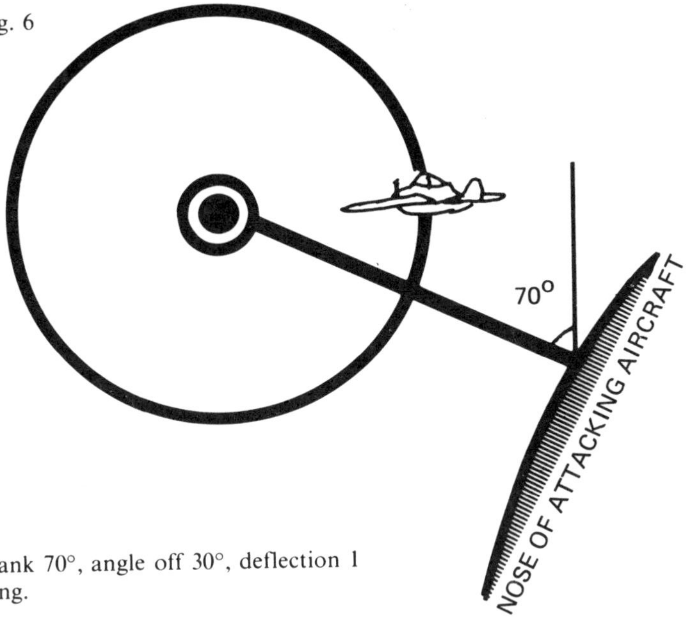

Bank 70°, angle off 30°, deflection 1 ring.

Fig. 7

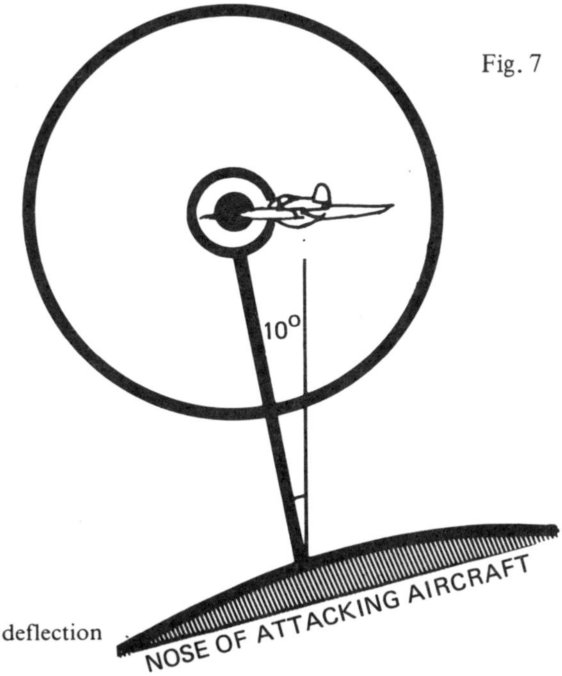

Bank 10°, angle off 10°, deflection 0.3 rings.

One tries to fly as smoothly as possible, but avoiding manoeuvres by the target often make this difficult and some ham-fisted work can be necessary, for example, when you've turned in to the target too late and the deflection is increasing so rapidly that the G forces build up to a very high level and he's still flying away out of your gunsight, in which case an immediate closing of your own throttles can result in enough loss of speed to enable you to increase the *angular* rate of turn and get the sight bearing again. It can also, of course, result in a high-speed stall, which takes you out of the battle for a while.

Our .303 ammunition wasn't much use beyond a range of 200 yards and we had a rough-and-ready system of range estimation in that the wing span of the heavier stuff that we dealt with just about filled the diameter of the outer ring at 200 yards. A fighter filled about half the diameter, though this was normally of academic interest only as I never experienced a situation where a fighter was foolish enough to overshoot after his attack and allow me a shot at him with the front guns. A further factor which tended to reduce one's accuracy, though not mentioned in the gunnery manuals, was return fire from the target, of course.

Tracer ammunition was designed to help in aiming. The base of a tracer bullet had a pellet of a compound which was ignited in the barrel of the gun by the flame of the propellant and this showed up as a red dot arcing up into the line of sight from the guns (in our case) two feet below the sight, to zero at 200 yards. For reasons which would take too long to go into, tracer could be a mixed blessing. I, for one, found it too easy to miss ahead of the target if you relied on it too much. At this stage of the war, our guns were belted up in the sequence of two ball, one tracer, two armour-piercing, one incendiary so we shot off about seven tracers a second from our two guns. These showed up as a scattering of red dots around the inner ring of the sight; but just *where,* along the trajectory, those red dots were, could be difficult to estimate.

So perhaps you will understand why, although we belted out forty rounds a second from our front pair of Brownings, we didn't necessarily hit an awful lot.